How Should We Then Live?

JAY R. LEACH

iUniverse, Inc.
New York Bloomington

How Should We Then Live?

iUniverse books may be ordered through booksellers or by contacting:

iUniverse
1663 Liberty Drive
Bloomington, IN 47403
www.iuniverse.com
1-800-Authors (1-800-288-4677)

ISBN: 978-1-4502-3830-4 (sc)
ISBN: 978-1-4502-3831-1 (ebook)

Printed in the United States of America

iUniverse rev. date: 7/6/2010

All Scripture passages were taken from the New King James Version of the Holy Bible except where noted.

DEDICATION

This book is dedicated to the Church of our Lord and Savior, Jesus Christ, around the World. It is intended to contribute to a Biblical world view; so that each reader may realize their purpose (ministry) in the overall plan of God for man. And as a result, individuals, families, and communities may be transformed for Christ. The author does not benefit through royalties from the proceeds of the sale of this book. All proceeds are reinvested through the Bread of Life Ministries for the furtherance of the Gospel and kingdom of our Lord, Jesus Christ.

ACKNOWLEDGMENTS

To my darling wife, of 47 years, Magdalene, who is also my partner in ministry I am grateful to her for her love, understanding, and patience with me; as I disappeared into my study for hours of preparation. She has taught me much about life, love, and the Lamb. Without her support, I would never have attempted to put these ideas into print. To the students of the Bread of Life Bible Institute and to the ministers and members of the Bread of Life Church & Ministry Fellowship, and the Bread of Life Christian Center who have been sounding boards and refiners of these ideals .To the churches to whom God has privileged me to pastor over the past 30 years, I thank you. Many of the principles contained in this book were birthed out of our quest to be spiritual disciple-makers. To our children, grandchildren, and great grandchildren, whose tender spirits have humbled me before a holy and gracious God; who has allowed me to live and see them grow and become saved and sanctified ministers in their own right. Truly, I give God all of the glory!

INTRODUCTION

The major reason for writing this book is found in a word that moves around like an old man's blood vessel – the word is "truth!" It is amazing to observe the various secular professionals at work today. Each seems to operate in his or her definition of the word "truth."

A look across the spectrum of churches reveals something similar to the secular in two respects. First, many have adopted a form that totally omits and denies the truths of God's Word and have set their own agenda. Their church business meeting resembles their secular counterpart in the fact that the latest secular advertisement ideas, innovations, methods, and results are tried and adopted into the church for membership growth and fund-raising.

In this country, truth is handicapped, because we seek it through the intellect, or science. However truth is not based on knowledge. Therefore, Christians should know that absolute truth cannot be obtained through these channels. Truth is based on a person, Jesus Christ; so, the knowing would be the results of experiencing Him. Jesus said, "..............*I am truth*.............." Therefore, if truth is found in a person, then no doubt that which is false must also be embodied by someone. Jesus points this out,

"You are of your father, the devil, and the desires of your father you want to do. He was a murderer from the beginning, and does

not stand in the truth, because there is no truth in him. When he speaks a lie, he speaks from his own resources, for he is a liar, and the father of it" (John 8:44).

Since it is a biblical fact that man is ruled by, and willingly follows the prince of darkness, who is the god of this world, naturally, he cannot distinguish truth from a lie. Since Jesus is Truth, man can only know truth through a relationship with Him. The Bible says, Adam *knew* his wife and she conceived a son Cain *knew* his wife and she conceived a son. We can see that this word "knowing" is relational, intimate. We see then, truth is not obtained intellectually (head), nor scientifically (experiment), but experientially (heart).

Darkness and lies go together; just as truth and light go together. In the Scripture, Jesus admonishes His followers to, ".........*take heed that no man deceive you.*" Why did He do this? He wanted to emphasize how deception, appears as if it is truth. We are so gullible for outward appearances in this nation; that we can easily be deceived. If it looks real but is false, sounds right but is wrong. It is received as truth, but in reality it is a lie. For example, watching the couple who crashed the President's State dinner, actually, they looked by their outward appearances more like they belonged than some on the guest list. However, they were a lie! Now how that case should be handled; and how it will probably come out will be a lesson for all to behold.

The disturbing fact is many of our church leaders are joining the deception; rather than combating it. I read an article on the training of Federal Treasury agents in reference to how they handle counterfeit money. The only thing they do with it is burn it. They have absolutely no use for counterfeit, in training young agents; because they use real money for training. The students are required to become so familiar with the real thing that feeling it or spotting the false is automatic. What a difference it would make if believers would study God's Word and develop a true relationship with the Lord – so that any deception would be picked up immediately. Again, this "knowing" is from an experience of the heart, an intimate relationship; and revelation not from the intellect only.

To be effective, we must learn to communicate with a culture that thinks we are outdated, useless, and opinionated. To be out there in the public square with tracts, and a personal testimony won't make much sense to a person who believes that there is no absolute truth; so to them truth is what the individual determine it to be.

What we are realizing is that truly without Christ; we can do nothing. One mark of so-called post modernism is its lack of stability, and attitudes toward old structures. So to cope with them; some churches have reversed "believe and belong" to "belong and believe." God forbid! When asked on the Day of Pentecost: What shall we do? The answer that the apostle Peter gave then still holds true today, *"Repent, everyone of you"* (SEE Acts 2:37-38)

The apostle Paul brought it all home for us in his prayer for the Gentiles, as the prisoner of Jesus Christ for them (SEE Ephesians 3:1; 14-19). He continues on his knees, ***"For this reason I bow my knees" (v.1).*** Note the specific purpose of his prayer. It addressed the Father of all believers in heaven and earth:

1. That the Father would strengthen you through His Spirit in the inner man (v.16).

2. That Christ may dwell in your hearts through faith (v.17).

3. That you be rooted and grounded in love (v. 17).

4. That you may be able to understand fully what God has done. Don't miss God's eternal plan. Grasp it!

5. That you may know the love of Christ ("know" by experiencing it) through a heart relationship with Him. (v.19).

6. That you may know that love passes knowledge (intellectual and scientific). Our faith is activated by love.

7. That you may be filled with all the fullness of God – that you experience all aspects of His truth and power (v.19).

"I pray we all experience this; before going forth.

Jay R. Leach, Bible Teacher

Contents

SECTION I

KINGDOM PERSPECTIVES
CHAPTERS 1 – 7

CHAPTER 1
NO LACK IN THE KINGDOM
("ABUNDANCE")

Many of us came up hearing the old hymn of the church, "I'll Fly Away." The blessing was understood to be in a land (God's Kingdom) – future and far away. However, God has revealed in His Word that the kingdom is here, present as well as future. Thus, His kingdom is on the earth, in fact it has invaded the earth and we are in the spearhead with Him in that kingdom invasion.

Absolute Abundance

To understand the Kingdom of heaven and our places in it as kingdom citizens; it is imperative that we understand how it holds sway over the visible world. We must fully understand two important points. First, there is no lack in the kingdom of God. Secondly, we can have total favor with the Ruler of the kingdom. Unlike a democracy, a kingdom has a king and that king bears the full responsibility for the sustenance, protection, and welfare of his citizens. The Scripture declares that we are in the world, but not of this world. Our world is the Kingdom of heaven. Having been "born again," we can realize the kingdom of heaven here and now. With that in mind, on the first point, Jesus, told His disciples that they were permitted to know the mysteries of the kingdom of heaven; but it is a total impossibility for the world to know them (SEE Matthew 13:11).The mysteries pertaining to the kingdom of Heaven are not referring to things that cannot be known; but to truths that are not revealed to you (the believer) until now.

We are admonished:

But seek first the kingdom of God and His righteousness, and all these things shall be added to you (Matthew 6:33).

The kingdom of God is the same as the kingdom of Heaven. He is urging us to seek salvation and a right relationship with the King. Your care and provision becomes His full responsibility (SEE Romans 8:32; Philippians 4:19; 1 Peter 5:7). On the second point, He sets forth the kingdom truth of "no lack – but abundance" with a parable of a sower. Parables were a common form of teaching, often cast in the form of a story. Jesus used parables to obscure the truth from unbelievers (probably an act of mercy lest their condemnation be increased); while making it clearer to His disciples. Here Jesus clearly establishes that the ability to comprehend spiritual truth is a gracious gift from God and given sovereignly to His children. Understanding the parable of the sower is the key to understanding how the kingdom of heaven and the Word of God works (SEE Matthew 13:11).

The Parable of the Sower

"Therefore hear the parable of the sower: When anyone hears the word of the kingdom, and does not understand it; then the wicked one comes and snatches away what was sown in his heart. This is he who received seed by the wayside.

But he who received the seed on stoney places, this is he who hears the word and immediately receives it with joy; yet he has no root in himself, but endures only for a while. For when tribulation or persecution arises because of the word, immediately he stumbles.

Now he who received seed among thorns is he who hears the word, and the cares of the world and the deceitfulness of riches choke the word, and he becomes unfruitful.

But he who received seed on the good ground is he who hears the word and understands it, who indeed bears, fruit and produces: some a hundredfold, some sixty, some thirty (Matthew 13:18-23).

Every preacher and teacher sows the Word, but the Holy Spirit of God is the One who quickens the seed (Word) that is sown (SEE 1 Peter 1:23). The four types of ground into which the seed (Word) is sown represents the heart. The condition of the ground (heart) determines the degree of understanding and receptivity (yield) of the Word sown.

Thinking of the *"wayside"* brings to mind, ground hardened or packed by frequent and high amounts of traffic. Therefore, the word (seed) sown into the hardened heart is not understood and snatched away by Satan.

The *"stony ground"* represents the heart that receives the word (seed) with joy; yet when tribulation or persecution comes because of the word, immediately, he falls away.

The *"thorny ground"* represents the heart that receives the word (seed); however, the cares of this world and the deceitfulness of riches choke the word, and he becomes unfruitful.

Notice, in the parable the *"good ground,"* which represents the teachable, understanding and hearing heart, yielded harvests of a hundredfold, sixty-fold, and thirty-fold. That is abundances of: 10,000%, 6000%, and 3000% as with a forest, maple tree, or sunset – it's more than enough.

Each of the four heart conditions are determined by the importance of the Word of God to the individual. Through the Word we receive the mind of Christ, that sees as God sees, that thinks God's thoughts after Him (SEE 1 Corinthians 2:12 – 14). To receive that abundance of the kingdom the word is quickened in our spirit by the Holy Spirit (SEE Luke 8:11; 1 Peter 1:23; James 1:18 and 1 Corinthians 4:15).

Because God is the only true free being in the universe, His kingdom is a sphere of total possibilities. Jesus demonstrated this with the little boy's lunch of two fish and five loaves in (SEE Matthew 14:16-21).

Consider this:

God is never fazed by circumstances.

Neither is He limited by His own universe or the natural laws He Himself established.

He can create from nothing, or He can take existing matter and transform it.

He is a total world – total health – total life – total energy – total strength – total provision.

In the matter of favor, Jesus was our perfect illustration of God's bestowal:

"And Jesus increased in wisdom and stature, and in favor with God and man" (Luke 3:22).

God presented the supreme Gift of this grace at the time of the baptism of Jesus in the River Jordan

"And the Holy Ghost descended in a bodily shape like a dove upon Him, and a voice came from heaven, which said, "Thou art my beloved Son; in thee I am well pleased" (Luke 3:22).

This, God the Father was saying, was the One He had spoken of and promised for centuries. He was going to pour out His grace and blessing on His only begotten Son and on those who belong to Him.

We need to recognize that when the Bible speaks of God's "grace" it is speaking of His "favor." In the New Testament, the Greek word for grace is "charis" perhaps best defined as "the unmerited favor of God." This favor the apostle Paul said, allows us to stand before God Himself. (SEE Ephesians 2:8 –18).

"For through Him we both have access by one Spirit to the Father" Eph. 2:18.

Think about it. If we have access to the Father, standing before Him in His favor, then we have the prospect of continuous blessing. Now when God blesses us and keeps us, and lets His face shine upon us, and is gracious to us (SEE Numbers 6:24-25).

1. Then before men we appear in a light that far transcends our natural abilities.

2. He can cause our plans to succeed.

3. He can cause people to like us.

4. He can cause us to be preferred and chosen above others of equal talents.

5. He can protect our children.

6. He can guard our property.

7. He can cause His angels to aid and guard us.

Therefore, we have favor with Him in the invisible world and the visible world. Now that we understand the two truths of no lack in the kingdom; and abundance of grace, we are ready for the fact that God has entered into a partnership with redeemed man.

CHAPTER 2
THE MISSING PIECE ("SAY IT")

Christ has given us the potential of cooperating with His Spirit in the whole work of the kingdom. Notice:

For if when we were enemies we were reconciled to God through the death of His Son, much more, having been reconciled, we shall be saved by His life (Romans 5:10). Therefore, my beloved, as you have always obeyed, not as in my presence only, but now much more in my absence, work out your own salvation with fear and trembling; for it is God who works in you both to will and to do for His good pleasure (Philippians 2:12-13).

We hear much about the church being in trouble today. We are the church. God saved us one at a time (individually). Therefore, as individuals like the Moon reflects the Sun; so should we reflect Christ; who resides in us. Right relationship with Christ enters us into a partnership with God.

Prayer

Prayer is the link between finite man and the infinite purpose of God. In its ultimate sense, prayer consists of hearing God's will and then doing it on earth. Prayer does not consist merely of asking for what we want. Martin Luther King Jr. stated that trying to live without praying is like trying to live without breathing. True prayer means to put our lives into total conformity with what God desires. How is that accomplished? We begin by dropping our own preconceived ideas (SEE Jeremiah 23:18). We enter His presence by grace and wait on Him. "Lord what do you want of me? What are you doing? One great man of faith said, "Have no mind of your own in the matter." In Mark's Gospel, Jesus, discussing the withered fig tree, said that the first thing required was faith in God. Yes, absolute trust and confidence that He is God almighty, unlimited and infinite (SEE Mark 11:12-14).Implied was the fact that God speaks to His people, revealing what He is doing. Then Jesus said,

For assuredly, I say to you, whosoever says to this mountain, "Be removed and cast into the sea, and does not doubt in his heart, but believes that those things he says will be done, he will have what he says (Mark 11:23).

If we fully believe God and have discerned His will, Christ said that we many translate that will from the invisible world to the visible by the spoken word (SEE Genesis 1:3).In other words, God uses the spoken word to translate spiritual energy, sheer power into the material (SEE John 1:3; Genesis 1:2).

Therefore I say to you, whatever things you ask when you pray, believe that you receive them, and you will have them (Mark 11:24)

.He took us right back to where He began. Have faith in God - know who He is - know what He is doing – trust His favor upon us – participate with Him. What we *say* in His name should then come to past.

Understanding Rhema and Logos

Let us therefore be diligent to enter that rest, lest anyone fall according to the same example of disobedience. For the word of

God is living and powerful, and sharper than any two-edged sword, piercing even to the division of soul and spirit, and joints and marrow, and is a discerner of the thoughts and intents of the heart. And there is no creature hidden from His sight, but all things are naked and open to the eyes of Him to whom we must give account (Hebrews 4:11- 13).

This text is among the most prominent in understanding faith's call to "speak" or "confess" the Word of God. The passage relates to Israel's rejection of God's promise; which resulted in a whole generation dying in the wilderness and failing to possess the inheritance God had for them. The Bible here describes itself: *"The word of God is living and powerful."* The term for "word" in the Greek is *"logos"* which commonly refers to the expression of a complete idea and is used in referring to the written Holy Scriptures. It contrasts with *"rhema"* which refers to a word spoken or given. When you are facing a situation of need, trial, or difficulty, the promises of God may become a "rhema" to you; that is, a weapon of the Spirit, "the word of God" (SEE Ephesians 6:17).It's authority is that this "word" comes from God's Word. Its immediate significance is that He has "spoken" it to your spirit by His Spirit and is calling forth faith just as He did for Israel when He directed them toward their inheritance. This spoken word or "rhema" stands firm in the promises of the "logos" – the completed Word of God – the Bible. (SEE Philippians 2:9-11; Hebrews 11:13-14).

The Missing Piece

For the majority of Christians throughout history, the *"speaking"* has been the missing piece between what we believe and what we do. We have lost the understanding of how we are to work once we enter into the *unobstructed view of God* that Jesus provides in the kingdom. (SEE Revelation 1:1-20).

Sin Clouds Our View

But once sin is forgiven – we enter boldly into the throne room of grace and commune with God by the Spirit, who communicates with our spirit. It's like tuning into a radio or television station. Get on the right frequency and the station comes in loud and clear. So it is with listening to the Lord. He is speaking constantly, but we are often on the wrong frequency.

Once He has spoken to us, we are to speak after Him; if we do, miracles happen! If we don't nothing usually happens. In the material world, God has chosen to enter into partnership with us, His co-laborers; who He is grooming for His perfect, visible kingdom on the earth.

One must die to (the flesh) self and anything else that clouds his or her view of Christ. Living in harmony with Christ, and receiving His thoughts – we speak after Him in the manner of Ezekiel in the vision of the valley of dry bones (SEE Ezekiel 37:4, 7-10).

God said,

"So shall My word be that goes forth from My mouth; It shall not return to Me void, but it shall accomplish what I please, And it shall prosper in the thing for which I sent It" (Isaiah 55:11).

God's Word performs His purpose.

CHAPTER 3
HAVE FAITH IN GOD
("THE 6TH SENSE")

As I have emphasized in prior chapters, the covering statement for the entire matter of the Kingdom is "Have faith in God."

WHAT IS FAITH?

Faith governs all, but it is frequently misunderstood. To properly live an abundant and victorious life in this world – citizens of the kingdom must fully understand it. Faith in the kingdom of God is to the kingdom citizens; what money is to citizens of this world. The Bible says bluntly,

The just shall live by faith (Hebrews 10:38).

Now faith is the substance of things hoped for, the evidence of things not seen. For by it the elders obtained a good testimony. By faith we understand that the worlds were framed by the word of God, so that the things which are seen were not made of things which are visible. (Hebrews 11:1-3).

But without faith it is impossible to please Him; for he who comes to God must believe that He is, and that He is a rewarder of those who diligently seek Him (Hebrews 11:6).

Said another way, faith is the title deed to things we can't see. When we buy property, we meet with the seller and papers are drawn up. We receive a deed and it says we own a stated piece of property. We don't have to go to it – we don't have to see it – it's ours. We have a title deed. It's the same with faith. We have a title deed to what God has promised. Our role is to believe in our hearts that it has been accomplished, according to what God has given us the deed to – and speak it!

We can't force it – we can't work it up. We can receive it only from God.

"As it is written, the just shall live by faith" (Romans 1:17).

Paul intends to prove that it has always been God's way to justify sinners by grace on the basis of faith *alone*. God established Abraham as a pattern of faith – and thus calls him the father of all who believe (SEE Romans 4:11, 16, 22-25; Galatians 3:6,7). Elsewhere, Paul uses this same phrase to argue that no one has ever been declared righteous before God except by faith alone (SEE Galatians 3:11), and that true faith will demonstrate itself in action (SEE Philippians 2:12, 13).This last expression emphasizes that true faith is not a single event, but a way of life – it endures.

That endurance is called the perseverance of the saints.

Notice, *And you, who once were alienated and enemies in your mind by wicked works, yet now He has reconciled in the body of His flesh through death, to present you holy, and blameless, and above reproach in His sight if indeed you continue in the faith, grounded and steadfast, and are not moved away from the hope of the gospel which you heard, which was preached to every creature under heaven, of which I Paul became a minister (Colossians 1:21-23).*

Christ's substitutionary death on the cross paid the full penalty for the sin of all who believe; and made reconciliation possible and real (SEE 2 Corinthians 5:18-21; Romans 3:25; 5:9, 10; 8:3). Holy in His sight refers to our (believers) positional relationship to God. In Christ, now the believer is separated from sin and set apart to God by imputed righteousness. As a result of the believers union with Christ in His death, burial, and resurrection, God considers true believers as holy as His Son (SEE Ephesians 1:4-6).

The Bible says,

So then faith comes by hearing, and hearing by the Word of God (Romans 10:17).

We hear the Lord's Word – it builds in our hearts – and the light goes on. *"It's mine!"* Deep down inside, there will be no doubt. That's what the Lord meant when He referred in the fig tree episode to the one **whoever says to this mountain** and **does not doubt in his heart.** The mountain will move if the Lord has spoken (SEE Mark 11:23). Let me add a word to drive home the point. Our faith through out all of this must be in the Lord. Our faith is not to be in our faith. (SEE Matthew 17:20; 1 John 5:14-15).

Trust in the LORD with all your heart, and lean not on your own understanding, In all your ways acknowledge Him, and He shall direct your path (Proverbs 3:5-6).

CHAPTER 4
BE TRANSFORMED
("A RENEWED MIND")

The Importance of Right Thinking

Because our minds are the agents our spirits use in influencing the world around us – it is imperative; for us to realize that any negative thinking (attitudes) can tear down our best efforts. Unfortunately, some people glean a few of the truths of the kingdom of God; then they try to gain the kingdom without submitting themselves to the King. Some of the spiritual principles of the kingdom, taken by themselves, can produce some temporary benefits (SEE Matthew 16:26).

In Romans 12, the apostle Paul admonishes us to be not conformed; but to be transformed by the renewing of our minds. He is calling for a total commitment to God; which carries us beyond our initial acceptance of Christ as our Savior. This requires a personal separation unto God.

When we accepted Christ, the Holy Spirit quickened our Spiritually dead spirit, dead, as a result of Adam's sin. Prior to this quickening our spirit was out of the way; and our flesh or (soul comprising: mind, emotions, and will), took control of our being. **SEE APPENDIX I** for a full explanation.

We begin this process by "presenting" our most prized possession (our soul and physical bodies), a living sacrifice (no longer *dead* in sin), to God. "Holy" means separated from the world system, and in this case to God and His kingdom; which is expected of us.

I beseech you therefore, brethren, by the mercies of God, that you present your bodies a living sacrifice, holy acceptable to God, which is your reasonable service (12:1).

A separation *to* God requires a separation *from* the world. The world does not refer to this physical creation, but to the sphere of evil operating in our world under the dominion of Satan (SEE 1 John 4:4; 5:19; John 12:31; 14:30; 16:11).

This moves us to the next step of non-conformity with the world (system). The world then is the natural system of thinking and living which shapes the person into its idea. For example, before we are saved – the culture, and significant others have a profound influence in conforming or shaping the way we think, our habits, and the way we live; as they appeal to our five senses.

And do not be conformed to this world, but be transformed by the renewing of your mind, that you may prove what is that good and acceptable and perfect will of God. (Romans 12:2

Transformation requires a total change in our thinking (world view), attitudes and behavior. As sinners our world view was natural and shaped by the *kingdom* of this world; so now as believers our world view should be shaped (transformed) by our relationship with Christ and obeying through living out His Word. The world tells us that the power is within each of us to *"just do it,"* God knows that we cannot sufficiently motivate ourselves to deny the flesh and pursue separation or holiness on a daily basis. This thinking in the believer's life leads to the man in Romans 7; however, he must move on to Romans 8:1.

There is therefore now no condemnation to those who are in Christ Jesus, who do not walk according to the flesh, but according to the Spirit (v.1).

Walking according to the Spirit is proper action. According to Paul, our motivation to pursue transformation is found in the mercies of God. We do it out of a sense of appreciation for what the Lord has done for us. One great theologian expressed it well when he said, "If Jesus Christ is God and died for me, then no sacrifice can be too great for me to make for Him."

But why does the Lord want you to choose to present yourself to Him and then move on through to transformation? The answer

"Do you not know that your body is the temple of the Holy Spirit who is in you, whom you have from God, and you are not your own? For you were bought at a price; therefore glorify God in your body And in your spirit which are God's" (1 Corinthians 6:19-20).

The sum of contemporary thinking and values form the moral atmosphere of the world and is always dominated by Satan.

The Scripture says,

"Whose minds, the god of this age has blinded, who do not believe, lest the light of the gospel of the glory of Christ, who is the image of God, should shine on them" (2 Corinthians 4:4).

Thoughts, ideas, speculations, reasoning, philosophies, and false religions are the ideological forts in which men barricade themselves against God and the gospel (SEE 1 Corinthians 3:20).

The Greek word for transformed is *"metamorphosis"* which connotes a change in outward appearance. Matthew uses the same word to describe the Transfiguration (SEE Matthew 17:2).

Christ briefly and in a limited way displayed outwardly His *inner* divine nature, and glory at the Transfiguration, Christians must manifest their inner redeemed natures, not once, however, but 24/7, again, our reasonable service. I believe this is the most effective evangelism tool for the individual and the local churches in this post-modern world. (SEE 2 Corinthians 3:18; Romans 5:10; Ephesians 5:18).

That kind of transformation, and renewal of mind can occur only as the Holy Spirit changes our thinking through consistent study and meditation of God's Word (SEE Psalm 119:11; Colossians 1:28; 3:10, 18; Philippians 4:8).

The renewed mind is one saturated with and controlled by the Word of God. The good and acceptable and perfect will of God results from living out the application of the word studied, meditated upon, and incarnated into others. These words are borrowed from Old Testament sacrificial language and describe a life that is morally and spiritually spotless, just as the sacrificial animals were to be (SEE Leviticus 22:19-25).

The divine undeserved favor that called Paul to be an apostle and gave him spiritual authority, also produces sincere humility and will lead believers to recognize that in themselves they are nothing (SEE 1 Timothy 1:12-24; 1 Peter 5:5).

Therefore, right thinking, resulting from a renewed mind will more often than not result into successful action. Remember, a renewed mind requires a change of world view; which can be achieved only through a right relationship with Christ and His Word. (SEE Matthew 6:33).

Many sincere followers of Jesus Christ destroy their effectiveness in the world because they don't understand the laws of authority; for example "the power of what they say." Solomon wrote:

A man shall eat well by the fruit of his mouth, but the soul of the unfaithful feeds on violence (Proverbs 13:2).

In other words, when you speak blessing, favor, victory, and success, these things come to you. But sadly, the majority of Christians ignore this truth.

"How do you feel?" *Reply:* "I feel terrible" – not realizing he or she has just commanded his or her body to be sick.

"Can you do it" *Reply:* "I can't do that," – not knowing that he or she has limited God and themselves by their words.

I can't get out of debt," someone says – he or she has just commanded their debts to continue.

We call such negative assertions "being real" about the situation. But they aren't realistic; for they ignore the power of God. Pettiness, majoring in minors, fear of failure, constant complaining, murmuring, criticism, -- all inhibit the realization of kingdom conditions.

As a man thinks in his heart, so is he (Proverbs 23:7).

CHAPTER 5
FAITH AND GRACE (BALANCE)

In the course of my teaching in the Bread of Life Bible Institutes around the country, one of the most frequent questions I'm asked is, "Please tell me what's keeping me from receiving the promised blessings of God? They continue, "I have been praying, reading my Bible, going to church, and faithfully paying my tithes, yet I don't seem to get a breakthrough or my prayers answered."

These folks have fallen into the false teaching or belief of linking God's response to their prayers and circumstances; as if His approval or disapproval depends on their performance. The problem here is a misunderstanding of the proper relationship between grace and faith. These two should remain in balance for a proper response from our King.

Certainly, we have little problem understanding the definition of "grace" as the unmerited, unearned, undeserved favor of God. Knowing this, we fail to understand that *grace has nothing to do with us.*

Grace existed before you ever came to be. If grace is unearned and undeserved; then it has to be of *God and it's His part in the equation.* **Faith** is defined as being our acceptance of what God has <u>already</u>

provided us by grace, or faith only provides what God has already provided for you. Therefore, *faith is your part in the equation.*

Grace and faith work together, and as the two sides of an equation must be in balance.

The Scripture says,

For by grace you have been saved through faith, and that not of yourselves; it is gift of God, not of works, lest anyone should boast (Ephesians 2:8-9).

Many times people hear something; whether it is actually interpreted correctly or not, it becomes so familiar that they believe it to be true; as they heard it. This Scripture clearly states that we are saved by grace through faith, not one or the other. Listen, **grace is what God does and faith is what we do.** It takes both working together to *receive* salvation.

If salvation came by grace alone, everyone would be saved; for God's grace is provided to all men. Paul admonishes,

For the grace of God that brings salvation has appeared to all men (Titus 2:11).

Our blessings are past tense – always. God has already brought the gift of salvation to everyone through Jesus Christ. However, it is by faith that a person receives what was provided 2000 years ago. For example we know there is water in the pipe, but until we open the faucet, the water will remain in the pipe. The message that much of the church is preaching today causes us to become conscious of sin instead of conscious of righteousness. It also causes us to link our performance to all the other blessings of God (SEE Romans 3:19-20).

God's grace not only provided for salvation 2000 years ago; but also for every need of your life. That provision is not based on whether you are reading the Bible enough, praying enough, going to church, or even paying your tithes.

Before you ever had a financial need – God had already made provision.

Before you were sick – God, through grace, provided your healing (SEE 1 Peter 2:24).

Before you ever became discouraged – God blessed you with all spiritual blessings. (SEE Ephesians 1:3).

God anticipated every need you could ever have and has met those needs through Jesus Christ before you existed. Now! That's grace.

What God provided by grace 2000 years ago now becomes a reality when mixed with faith. Faith appropriates what God has already provided. Faith doesn't move God; He isn't stuck over your problem. Faith doesn't make God do anything. Thus, *grace* and *faith* work together – our part is to accept what God has already done. Again, grace and faith must work together.

Therefore, the premise that God is to blame for disasters, poverty, or sickness can't be true; because the Scriptures clearly ascertain this to Satan. Satan is the author of evil. It is Satan who comes to steal, kill, and destroy (SEE John 10:10; 1 Peter 5:8; 1 John 3:8).

Jesus said,

"I have come that they may have life, and that they may have it more abundantly (John 10:10).

As you give your total self to God, God gives His total self to you. That is the supreme message of the Bible. Inherent in God's "total self" of His own person is true, Bible-based prosperity – the real possibility of health for your total being (body, soul and spirit), and your material needs being met. Above all, His prosperity brings eternal life.

Jesus said that He came to give life ("Zoe" everlasting life) – not just ordinary existence, but life in fullness, abundance, and prosperity:

Beloved, I pray that you may prosper in all things and be in health, just as your soul prospers (3 John 2).

It is clear that God wants His children to prosper. How can anyone deny that? However, prosperity should not be the end in itself. It ought to be the result of a quality of life, commitment, dedication, and action that is in line with God's Word and His will. In this text the word "prosper" literally means "to help on the road" or "succeed in reaching." It clearly implies that divine prosperity is not a momentary, passing phenomenon, but rather it is an on-going, progressing state of success and well-being. It is intended for every area of our lives: the spiritual, the physical, the emotional, and the material. However, God does not want us to unduly emphasize any one area. We must maintain a balance.

God is pleased when His servants prosper:

Let them shout for joy and be glad, who favor my righteous cause; And continually, let the Lord be magnified, Who has pleasure in the prosperity of His servant (Psalm 35:27).

CHAPTER 6
MORE THAN RELIGION
("CHRISTIANITY").

There is something which makes Christianity more than a religion, more than an ethic, more than just a dream. It is this something that makes it relevant to each one of us right now, as a contemporary experience. It is this fact that Christ Himself is the very life content of the Christian life. Notice:

He who calls you is faithful, who also will do it (1 Thessalonians 5:24).

The One who calls you is the One who does that to which He calls you.

The One who calls you to a life of righteousness is the One who by your consent lives the life of righteousness through you, by His Spirit.

The One who calls you to minister to the needs of humanity is the One who by your consent ministers to the needs of humanity through you, by His Spirit.

The One who calls you to go into all the world and preach the gospel to every creature, is the One who by your consent, goes into all the world and preaches the Gospel to every creature through you.

For it is God who works in you both to will and to do His good pleasure (Philippians 2:13).

Christ Himself is the very dynamic of all He demands.

In Romans 5:10 we read:

For if when we were enemies we were reconciled to God through the death of His Son, much more, having been reconciled, we shall be saved by His life (Romans 5:10).

The Lord Jesus Christ therefore ministers to us in two distinct ways: He reconciles you to God by His death (SEE also 1 Peter 2:24; 3:19). He saves you by His life.

How?

Those that come to Him and believe on Him enter into a unique relationship with Him – they dwell in Him and He dwells in them (SEE John 6:56).

As Jesus lived by the Father, so are you to live by Him (v. 57).

How does Jesus live it? He said,

"Verily, verily I say unto you, The Son can do nothing of Himself" (John 5:19; see also 8:28).

Here we see Jesus Christ as man living in total dependence upon the Father. In other words, you can do no more without Him than he could do without the Father (SEE John 15:5).How much could the Father do through the Son? Everything! He was available to all that the Father made available to Him (SEE John 13:3; Colossians 1:19).

How much then can Jesus do through you and me? Everything! He is limited only by the measure of our availability to all that He makes available to us for,

"For in Him dwells all the fullness of the Godhead bodily. And you are complete in Him, who is the Head of all principality and power (Colossians 2:9-10).

How can you be saved by His life, as you have already claimed to be redeemed by His death? The answer is simple:

The just shall live by faith (Romans 1:17).

Faith that takes God precisely at His Word! Faith that simply says, "Thank you."

CHAPTER 7
TRUTH ("CHRIST")

Knowing God enables the Christian to affirm that there is absolute truth, an ultimate reality that begins with God and extends throughout His creation. The Christian can know truth (the way things really are) through two kinds of revelation.

Biblically speaking a mystery is not something that can't be known but a truth that has not been revealed until now. The two kinds of revelation of truth are:

General revelation – this truth is revealed through nature or creation. God communicates through creation. For example the sunrise and sunset is the same daily .The four seasons are in the same order each year. All that is visible points to the Almighty God. All men share this truth – admit it or not.

Special revelation – this truth is gained through the Bible (Logos) or by the Holy Spirit of God speaking directly into our spirit (Rhema). Simply put, revealed truth is the rock on which the Church stands or falls. The Bible is the ultimate authority for all Christians.

God could not have spoken something that is not true because that would be contrary to His nature. The transforming power of the

Bible affects people from all walks of life. The story is told of one page of John's gospel being left on an island in the Pacific during the great missionary era. Upon visiting the island three years later it was revealed that all the adult citizens of the island had converted to Christianity.

Jesus teaches that reality is not what we subjectively make of it, or what our culture may believe about it. There is objective truth and we are able to get it. Jesus is the ultimate reality. An atheistic worldview has gripped our culture; statistics from a recent A Barna report show that 63% of Americans deny the knowability of moral truth.

Among teenagers only 8% acknowledge there is moral truth. As we'll see in a later chapter, even serious Christians are being taken in. If this is the state of the church and the Christian family, we are truly in trouble. The church remember is "the pillar and foundation of the truth" (SEE 1 Timothy 3:15). But if we are intimidated by political correctness, the secular worldview along with the myth that all religions are alike; and all ways lead to God – who then shall be able to stand and defend the truth?

The Drift from Truth

In spite of all the many resources made available through our churches today; many of our young Christians have become impatient. They see us falling more and more into the trap of "cultural conformity." However, these young Christians have been formed by our postmodern age. If something conforms to fact or reality, it is considered to be true. The question we must ask is, "How do we know what is fact and actual reality?" God created the world. He also created laws which allow it to operate correctly. He also created man with a system of laws within which man was to operate in the perfect will of God. These laws are based of God's *ultimate truth*. God knows the truth of the matter. He created what is fact and reality. We can never know the facts of life outside of knowing God. Mere man cannot understand reality connecting with the perfect reality that God created. When something lines up with ultimate factual reality, it can be considered truth.

Two Kind of Reality

I read a story about a boy whose parents in his early childhood told him that a crooked line is straight and a goat is a cow; whenever he saw a goat he would call it a cow; and the same with the crooked line. He'd call the crooked line straight. When he went to school he found out that his parents had painted a false picture of reality; they did not tell him the truth and he began life with a false paradigm. Many have been sold this bill of goods by the god of this world and they are convinced that they know the truth. But it is not true! This is what has happened in the world; man has been deceived to believe things that are not fact. Sadly, many local churches are buying in on this same deception.

As stated above, there are two kinds of reality – (1) the reality that you live in, and (2) *God's reality (the ultimate reality and truth).* When our realty meshes or conforms to God's reality, life functions best. True believers are responsible for making things right, that is, to show people what a straight line actually is – by revealing the ultimate reality (God's reality).

It is our responsibility to show those in our sphere of influence how life is supposed to be, not just in words, but in character and lifestyle. We use the Bible as the guide to the ultimate way of living and reality – and line up our worldview accordingly.

The Bible tells us:

Now it shall come to pass, if you diligently obey the voice of the Lord your God, to observe carefully all His commandments which I command you today, that the Lord your God will set you on high above all nations of the earth (Deuteronomy 28:1).

In the U.S. military there is a book called the Uniformed Code of Military Justice – listed in this book are possible offenses that a soldier may commit and the appropriate punishment. Knowing the contents of this book encourages proper character and lifestyle. The Bible, differs from the Uniformed Code above in that it actually teaches us how to live and paints a picture of what life could be like if we obey God's ultimate design for us. It says in our text above that if we obey God's way of life then we will be blessed. It is not that God wants to punish us if we do not obey; rather, He knows what we must do to reach our full potential and to make a positive impact on our world for His glory. Ultimate reality, God's reality, is truth and it will never change.

Characteristic of Truth

The fundamental characteristic of truth is its (consistency meaning cohesiveness, firmness, agreement or harmony in parts or of different things, inherent, made up of). It is final and absolute. Circumstances cannot change truth. If circumstances causes you to re-think previous conclusions, and if honesty, in the light of new information, compels you to change convictions – it does not mean that truth has changed – it simply means that you never knew the truth, and that circumstance or additional information are compelling you to recognize the fact. Watch your comments and counsel (SEE Matthew 16:21-23).

In His prayer to the Father for those who believe on Him, the Lord Jesus said,

"Sanctify them by Your truth, Your Word is truth (John 17:17).

Truth is not academic. It is the ultimate principle of life, and sanctification is this principle in action. Truth obeyed in the human heart identifies the believer instantly with Christ Jesus.

Jesus said,

"Everyone who is of the truth hears My voice" (John 18:37).

And again, *"If you abide in My word, you are My disciple indeed. And you shall know the truth, and the truth shall make you free" (John 8:31, 32).*

SECTION II

ENEMIES OF TRUTH
CHAPTERS 8 – 11

CHAPTER 8
THE SPIRIT OF ANTICHRIST

Eschatology is that aspect of biblical doctrine dealing with "last things" (from Greek *eschatos,* meaning "final").

Little children, it is the last hour; and as you heard that the Antichrist is coming, even now many antichrists have come, by which we know that it is the last hour (1 John 2:18).

The "last hour" was introduced by the First Coming of Christ (SEE Acts 2:17; Hebrews1:1; 2; 1 Peter 1:20).

At the end of this period the one known as the Antichrist will come (SEE 2 Thessalonians 2:3-9).

There are already many such persons at work in the world. John identifies "other antichrists" as the heretics (deceitful, destructive, divisive "believers") who withdrew from the church. John tells us that their withdrawal is the evidence that they never really shared in the life and fellowship of the church. This is a sign of the approaching "last hour"--- in which many oppose the kingdom of Christ (vv. 18-19).

Notice in the Scripture the term antichrist refers to a particular person prophesied in the Scripture, this one is plural and refers to many individuals. John uses the plural to identify and characterize the false teachers who were troubling his congregations because their false doctrine distorted the truth and opposed Christ (SEE Matthew 24:24; Mark 13:22; Acts 20:28-30).

As if John was warning the church in his account of them: *they went out from us v.19),* they came from our Christian community and communion." The most advance churches today have their apostates, *"For, if they had been of us, they would have continued with us (v. 19);* had the truth of God's Word been rooted in their hearts it would have kept them with us."

Those that apostatize from Christianity sufficiently indicate that, before, they are hypocrites. But this was done (or they went out) *that they might be made manifest that none of them were of us" (v.19).*

Some of these hypocrites must be manifested here, as evidence that they never really shared in the life and fellowship of the church; and also for their own shame – in their reduction to the truth. I believe that Satan has had to prepare an antichrist in every generation since Calvary; for he knows not "the hour." A check of history reveals many well-known heads of State, including some American Presidents, and other personalities were thought to be that one antichrist, prophesied. (SEE 2 Thessalonians 2:3-9).

Recent decades have proven this truth. We are living in a time when every effort is being made to remove Jesus Christ's name from all areas of the public square and the culture. Today is truly the day of the saints, in the fact that those of us who are true to our Lord will live a life before men that magnifies His glory. We know the Truth! Listen to the apostle John,

"But you have an anointing from the Holy One, and you know all things. I have not written to you because you do not know the truth, but because you know it and that no lie is of the truth (v.20, 21).

In contrast to these antichrists who claim superior knowledge, two characteristics mark the genuine Christians:

1. They possess the illuminating truth through the ministry of the Holy Spirit, who guards them from error and deception (SEE Acts 10:36; 2 Corinthians 1:21).

2. The Holy Spirit guides the believer into knowing "all things." True Christians have built-in lie detectors and persevere in the truth. (SEE Luke 4:34; Acts 3:14; John 14:26;16:3).

Those who remain in heresy and apostasy manifest the fact that they were never genuinely born again (v.19).Three characteristics mentioned of antichrists:

1. They are false teachers and deceivers, who have departed from the faithful (vv. 22, 26).

2. They arise from within the church and depart from true fellowship and lead people out as they go (v. 26).

3. They deny the faith (sound doctrine), anyone denying the true nature of Christ as He is presented in the Scripture is an antichrist. The denial of Christ also constitutes a denial of God Himself, who testified to His Son (SEE 1 John 4:3; 5:9; 2 Thessalonians 2:11; John 5:2-38;8-18)

But the anointing which you have received from Him abides in you, and you do not need that anyone teach you; but as the same anointing teaches you concerning all things, and is true, and is not a lie, and just as it has taught you, you will abide in Him (v.28).

The genuine believer's response to the antichrists is to "walk in the truth," i.e. persevere in faithfulness and sound doctrine (SEE vv. 20-21; 2 John 4; 3 John 4).

CHAPTER 9
FROM BELIEF TO UNBELIEF

One of the most challenging changes in the cultural or secular context for ministry is the position between belief and unbelief – being identified as legitimate. The term *agnosticism* was invented by Thomas Huxley in 1869 to identify that position. That position has become increasingly popular. Many famous men have helped to advance the acceptance of unbelief. Certainly this is not a new position. The so-called beauty and power of nature was identified over 100 years ago as a religious successor to Christianity. Many of the proponents of unbelief came from among the leading intellectuals of their day, and a number were clergymen who had moved from belief to unbelief. Institutions of higher learning were among the most effective in advocating that belief in God was a matter of personal choice, not a given for understanding the world in which we live.

Unbelief in the Christian Perspective

In recent years this shift from belief in God to an acceptance of unbelief has been diluted by another trend. This is sometimes described as *"faith in faith,"* rather than faith in a God, who is alive and at work in the world.

This trend has been nurtured by a recent wave of nonsectarian religious television programs and by numerous novels and nonfiction books that focus on spirituality and a person's spiritual journey but little or no reference to the Holy Trinity of the Christian faith.

Sad to say, it appears that the societal acceptance of unbelief as a legitimate option came to light first in America among intellectuals. Later it spread and became an acceptable option among middle and working class Americans. Researchers only recently have found that unbelief has become a legitimate option for Blacks.

The acceptance of unbelief as a legitimate option for every citizen and that new wave of "faith in faith" have radically changed the context for pastoral ministry from what it was in the middle of the last century. That is one reason why it is much more difficult to be an effective pastor today than it was fifty years ago.

Of course, I see these proponents of unbelief as the others that I have presented as antichrists. Unbelief certainly negates belief and unbelievers are out because the Scripture declares, speaking of God,

But without faith it is impossible to please Him, for he who comes to God must believe that He is, and that He is a rewarder of those who diligently seek Him (Hebrews 11:6).

The emphasis here is on *"He is,"* the true God. Genuine faith does not simply *believe* that a divine being exists, but that the God of Scripture is the *only* real and true God who exists.

Not *believing* that God exists is equivalent to calling Him a liar! (SEE Romans 8:15, 16; Galatians 4:6; Titus 1:2; Hebrews 6:18).

The apostle John wrote,

He who believes in the Son of God has the witness in himself; he who does not believe God has made Him a liar, because he has not

believed the testimony that God has given of His Son. And this is the testimony that God has given us eternal life, and this life is in His Son (1 John 5:10-11).

Two Things that Hinders

The Bible talks about two major things that keep Christ and His Word from being effective and accomplishing its purpose.

1. **Religious Tradition** – The Pharisees were criticizing Jesus for allowing His disciples to break Jewish tradition by not washing their hands before they ate (SEE Matthew 15:1-9; also Romans 3:4). *"Thus you have made the commandment of God of no effect by your tradition.....And in vain you worship Me, teaching as doctrine the commandments of men" (Matthew 15:6,9).*

2. **Unbelief** – Not believing the truth of God's Word, that God's Word means what it says and says what it means. It never fails to amaze me – the number of people who will tell you they believe the Bible is truth; and the media is not. However, they spend hours each day reading and listening to untruthful newspapers, TV , even personal opinion. Even though they believe the Bible is God's truth – they spend only a fraction of the time in the Bible in comparison to the media.

Three Types of Unbelief

Non-believers express their unbelief in one or all of the three types below:

1. IGNORANCE

   I don't know God because, I've never heard of Him.

2. WRONG TEACHING I don't believe in miracles because I was taught that miracles ended when the last apostle died. Some are even taught that miracles are of the devil.

3. NATURAL THOUGHTS

It is God's will that I be sick; because I prayed – and when I went back to the doctor my illness had grown worse.

How do I pray for a Miracle (Matthew 17:20)

Praying for a miracle is welcoming a gift of the Holy Spirit to manifest. When we know God (experientially!), His will is to work one, He will witness that to your heart. Then you can ask Him to perform the miracle that you know He wants to bring about.

God has given us authority over disease, demons, sickness, storms, and finances (SEE Matthew 10:1; Luke 10:19). Many times we keep asking and He is calling us to exercise that authority by --- a "rhema" spoken word (SEE Chapter 2).

We are now coming to the end of another Hurricane season. A couple of years ago, I encouraged the Church where I pastor and our thirteen Bible Institute campuses to pray that the hurricanes would turn before hitting the east coast of America – then turn north into the open sea not hitting any nation. Then; as it happens – testify that God heard and answered your prayer! Of course, the skeptic will say, "many people prayed, how do you, know that God heard and answered your prayer?" It happened! Similarly, "in the name of Jesus," we command needed funds come to us, that demons come out, that affliction leave, command a sickness to depart. Jesus said,

"Whoever says to this mountain, 'Be removed and cast into the sea, 'and does not doubt in his heart, but believes that those things he says will be done, he will have what he says" (Mark 11:23).

KEY: Believe in your heart that it has already happened! God has given us the grace

So, we must add our faith with the anointing of God, then speak it forth! But remember, miracles come by faith in God's power – not by rituals, willpower or other works of humanity.

Mary's miraculous Conception

"Then Mary said to the angel, "How can this be, since I do not know a man?" (Luke 1:34).

And the angel answered and said to her, "The Holy Spirit will come upon you, and the power of the Highest will overshadow you; therefore, also, that Holy One who is to be born will be called the Son of God" (v.35).

Then Mary said, "Behold the maidservant of the Lord! Let it be to me according to your word."(v. 35).

Mary was in an extremely embarrassing and difficult position. Betrothed to Joseph, she faced the stigma of unwed mother. Joseph would obviously have known that the child was not his. She knew she would be accused of adultery –an offense punishable by stoning (SEE Deuteronomy 22:13-22; John 8:3-5). *"Let it be according to your will"* **(BOOM!),** she was pregnant. When she *spoke* in total faith, willingly and graciously submitted to the will of God – immediately, she was pregnant!

CHAPTER 10
DECPTION: SATAN'S TACTIC

The Scriptures reveal both good angels and evil angels. Their minds and understanding have been covered with the horrible darkness of *deception.* The same tactic Satan uses to lead his victims astray. Revelation 12:9 says, "... he deceives the whole world."

Satan operates this deception both in the realm of *truth* and in the realm of *power.* Proper ministry then must have a balance of the proclamation of doctrinal truth and demonstration of God's power.

Some try to limit the activity of demons to a few periods in history and to limit the power of the Holy Spirit against them to the Apostolic Era. Even the secular arena recognizes and has given voice to demonic activity – however, with their many claims of demonic activities worldwide, little is said of the divine power of the Holy Spirit.

The Root of Deception

To understand the spiritual warfare going on today – we need to understand where Satan came from and what motivates him. It is almost impossible to understand that a being who one of the most powerful of the angels (perhaps responsible for the very throne of God) could be so envious of God and his position in conjunction with God's, that he develops an insatiable desire to become a God like the Creator.

He did not become a glorious being like God – but rather he became a being who embodies all that is evil and ungodly, even though he still presents himself as an angel of light (SEE 2 Corinthians 11:14).

Even with his decision to challenge God over the issue of glory – God did not strip Lucifer of his power as an angel, nor did Lucifer give up his lust for glory. In fact this lust for glory seemed to intensify to the point where his primary purpose is to deprive God of all the glory he can.

He does this by working in the *thinking* and *experience* of God's children – His children by *creation* and His children by *redemption*. Jesus said,

"You are of your father the devil, and the desires of your father you want to do. He was a murderer from the beginning, and does not stand in the truth, because there is no truth in him. When he speaks a lie, he speaks from his own (resources), for he is a liar and the father of it (John 8:44).

He does this by telling them lies – something he is more than willing to do and by deceiving them through his shows of power (SEE Matthew 13:38; 1 John 3:8-10, 15; 2:16; Jude 6).We meet Satan, as he has come to be called, in the Garden of Eden where he comes on the scene to begin his war on God by attacking His children, Adam and Eve. He says to Eve "Has God indeed said, "You shall not eat of every tree of the garden?" *That's a lie. I'm here to tell you the truth. {A Leach interpretation, obviously} The fact is, God is holding out on you. You can't trust Him. Listen now, if you eat of that tree, you'll discover your true potential, namely that you are like God and really don't need Him to tell you what to do and not to do."* (SEE Genesis 3:1-7 for correct reading).

Notice how quick and clever Satan is in his deception. He reverses his role and the role of God. God became a liar and Satan became a truth-teller. Satan has developed quite an array of tricks to impress and lead people astray.

These tricks include clever lies, to which he has found humanity quite susceptible, and displays of power, which brings an equal response from us – especially when we have lost touch with the power of God.

The Nature of Deception

Deceiving is a most effective weapon of Satan. When we are deceived, we are thoroughly convinced that what we believe is true. Because of our insecurities – we are constantly looking for something solid and safe; therefore, making us vulnerable to a voice of authority. Satan speaks as a voice of authority.

Another trick involved in deception that Satan uses effectively is that none of us respond happily when told that we have been gullible and acting on a falsehood. We don't want our belief system challenged.

A very apparent deception many are falling for today especially in the marketplace is the idea that I am beyond temptation in some area – that I could not be deceived. I have people tell me, after falling into gross immorality, that they thought they were beyond such things.

Accountability is so very important. Everyone needs a friend, a true friend who will be honest; who will tell you what you don't want to hear. It must be said! Satan loves to tell us how spiritual we are. The deception is Satin hides the fact that God often speaks to us through others in the Body of Christ – many times those whom we don't want to listen to.

Who's talking Now

The question arises, who do I hear speaking, Satan or me! Almost always it is both. Satan is always on the prowl, looking for those folks trapped in Romans 7. His specialty in such instances is to get us thinking we have the ability to run our own lives. He leads us to think that neither Satan nor God is really needed to help explain or solve the problem. Jesus constantly reminds us, "Without Me you can do nothing." Yet, even in Christian circles, we still try to leave Him out. Satan is pleased!

Deception in the area of Truth

Satan is also very effective by couching his deceptions within truth. The Scripture speaks of the "doctrines of demons" (SEE 1 Timothy 4:1). He will speak the truth if it serves his purpose to deceive. For instance, in the wilderness temptation of Jesus, he said, "If You are the Son of God change these stones into bread" (Luke 4:3).

John tells us that demons don't like to make this confession – however, they will if it will help set up the deception (1 John 4:1-3).

I recall a group with a very gifted ministry especially in the gift of counsel. They began in the Bible, but eventually began to get into immorality – because of the anxiousness for a solution to their problems – the counselees became victims, even though the messages were no longer Scriptural.

CHAPTER 11
RELATIVISM

The so-called freedom revolution of the 60's rises up to haunt us daily. Many old terms have lost their meaning. Words such as love, gay, and truth have been redefined – giving rise to new terminology, one such term is relativism. Relativism is the theory that "there is no objective standard by which *truth* may be determined, so that truth varies with individuals and circumstances." This "baby" born out of the revolution began in academia; is now full-grown; and has reached critical mass in all areas of our society – even the church!

The claim of this revolution is that all truth is subjective. So if all truth is subjective – then what we know as "objective truth" is dead. If relativism were true, or accepted as true, society at large would be arrested by contradictory situations. Suppose I say, there is a spare tire in the trunk of the car" and you say "there is not a spare tire in the trunk of the car" – and we both are right, then there must be and not be a spare tire in the trunk of the car right now, at the same time. That is impossible!

Some argue that "if truth is relative, then no one is ever wrong – even when they are. As long as something is true to me, then I'm right even when I'm wrong.

A problem we face as ministers of the Gospel today is, how do our listeners view our sermons and teaching? Many who have been exposed to relativism through education and societal pressures – and not balanced with similar amounts of sound biblical knowledge; would probably consider what we preach and or teach – just our opinion.

Moral Relativism

Moral relativism is relativism applied to the morals of a society. First, what is a society? Webster defines society as (1) a voluntary association of persons for common ends; (2) a part of a community bound together by common interests and standards.

To be sure, from this definition, it is difficult to determine what the relevant society is. If a person from one society is cohabiting with a person from another society, then a person from a third society moves in next door; that holds a different view than the other two, which is the relevant society for determining whether this living arrangement is right or wrong?

Moral relativism suffers from a problem known as reformer's dilemma. If moral relativism is true, then it is logically impossible for a society to have a virtuous, moral reformer like Jesus Christ, Martin Luther King, Jr. or those of us who agree with and preach and teach the Word of God without compromise. Why? Moral reformers and true ministers are members of a society who stand outside that society's code and pronounce a need for reform and change in that code.

However, if an act is right if and only if it is in keeping with a given society's code, then the moral reformer himself is by definition an immoral person, *for his views are at odds with those of his society* .

I think that many of us do not realize the implication this could mean in reference to our pulpits and the truth of our convictions as God's messengers. By definition, we must always be *wrong* because our convictions go against the code of our society.

Some acts are wrong regardless of social convictions. Advocates of this persuasion usually adopt the standpoint of particularism and claim that all people can know that some things are wrong, such as sexual abuse of children, rape, stealing as such, and so forth, without first needing criteria for knowing how it is that they do, in fact, know such things.

Thus, an act of sexual abuse can be wrong and known to be wrong even if society says it is right, an act can be right and known as such even if society says it is wrong. In fact, an act can be right or wrong even if society says nothing whatever about that act. If normative relativism is true, there is nothing intrinsically right about the moral views in either of the societies represented above or any society for that matter. For this reason, moral relativism must be rejected.

What is Truth?

Dr. Francis Schaeffer called it "true truth" the idea that any particular thing can be known for sure – versus "truth" in the sense of something being my personal opinion. Relativism says, there are no absolutes, meaning no absolute truth.

Today society has lost the confidence that statements of fact can ever be anything more than just opinions; we no longer know that anything is certain beyond our own subjective thoughts. Secularly, then the word truth now means "true for me."

Over the last 40 years, these ideas have very subtly taken root – and they are very difficult to remove. Every part of truth dies including ethics, and morality dies with it. If truth cannot be known, then the concept of moral truth becomes blurred, ethics become relative, right and wrong become matters of individual opinion.

Because morality is reduced to personal tastes, people exchange the moral question: What *is* good? With the pleasure question: What *feels* good? When self-interest rules, it has a profound impact on behavior – especially affecting how we treat other people. Human dignity and respect depend on the existence of moral truth. Without it, there is no obligation of self-sacrifice on behalf of others. Instead, we can kick people to the curb when they become a burden, expensive, or begin to cramp our life styles. A young man cruised around the streets until he found just the right person – he pull out his pistol and killed a senior citizen, who was out for a walk. Asked why, he answered, "I was just bored!"

If there is no truth, nothing has transcendent value, including human beings. The death of morality reduces people to the status of mere animals. When people are viewed as things, they begin to be treated as things. We are witnessing a generation that has institutionalized moral relativism. The most subtle goal is to be *happy* and that justifies any means to that self-serving end. If this society rejects truth, why should we be surprised as we witness daily, the downward spiral of moral turbulence?

A statistic on a recent TV newscast reported that as of November, a total of 254 people randomly killed so far this year, 2009. No longer will we allow a hint of moral censure on sexual practices that were regarded as perverse only a generation ago. America like many other Western nations, take pride in its tolerance – yet tolerate no one who doesn't adhere to its moral open-mindedness. Gruesome newscasts compete with prime time shows – because it has become mere entertainment! We have become a numb nation!

The Culture of Offendedness

Christians face a very serous challenge today. A new and unprecedented right is now the central focus of legal, procedural and societal concern in many corridors, an offshoot of relativism – *a supposed right not to be offended.* It follows then, that since there are no absolutes; keep your criticisms of my beliefs to your self – so says America!

The risk of being offended has always been a part of what it means to live in a diverse culture that honors and celebrates free speech. A right to free speech means a right to offend; otherwise the right would need no protection.

This is a wake up call to Christians everywhere! We are admonished by Scripture not to compromise with the world. I believe this is about to happen to those of us who are not truly grounded in the word of God and walking in a right relationship with Him.

The secularists seem to be most intent on pushing a proposed right never to be offended by confrontation with the Christian, the truth of the Gospel, the Christian witness, or Christian speech and symbolism. This motivation lies behind the never-ending battle waged to remove all symbols, representations, references, and images related to Jesus Christ and Christianity from the public square.

A newscaster reported that just outside of San Diego, California on government property stands a large cross as a memorial – its very existence has become a major issue in the courts and now in Congress. Those pressing for the removal of the cross claim that they are *offended* by the fact that they are forced to see this Christian symbol from time to time.

Pastors, believers, do you see where this is going? This is working up to our very presence being an offense. Come Lord Jesus! We should note carefully that this notion of offendedness is highly emotional in character. In other words, those who now claim to be offended are generally speaking of an emotional state that has resulted from some real or perceived insult to their belief system – or from contact with someone else's belief system. In this sense, being offended does not necessarily involve any real harm but points instead to the fact that the mere presence of such an argument, image, or symbol evokes an emotional response of offendedness.

The distinguished Christian philosopher Paul Helm addresses this issue in an article published a few years ago in the summer edition of the *Salisbury Review,* published in Great Britain. He argues, "Historically, being offended has been a very serious matter. To be offended is to be caused to stumble so as to fall, to fail, to apostatize, to be brought down, to be crushed."

As evidence of this claim, He points to the language of the King James Bible in which Jesus says to His disciples:

"And if thy right eye offend thee, pluck it out, and cast it from thee: for it is profitable for thee that one of thy members should perish, and not that thy whole body should be cast into hell" (Matthew 5:29).

Likewise, Jesus also speaks a warning against those who would *"offend"* the *"little ones" (Matthew 18:6).*

Today – these desperate conditions are no longer required in order for an individual or group to claim the emotional status of offendedness. All that is required is often the vaguest notion of emotional dissatisfaction at what another has said, done, proposed, or presented.

This shift in the meaning of the word and its cultural usage is subtle but *extremely significant,* it also leads to inevitable conflict. People have always been upset by insensitive and negligent individuals – but the profile of offendedness, understood in this post-modern sense, is being pushed to the most extreme heights.

Now "the right never to be offended" is not only accepted as legitimate, but is actually promoted by the media, education, government, and by activist groups.

Given the mandate by Christ, our Savior to:

"Go therefore and make disciples of all nations, baptizing them in the name of the Father and of the Son and of the Holy Spirit, teaching them to observe all things that I have commanded you;

and lo, I am with you always, even to the end of the age" (Matthew 28:19-20).

We are to share the Gospel and to speak openly and publicly about Jesus Christ and the Christian faith. Christians must understand a particular responsibility to protect free speech and resist this culture of offendedness that threatens to shut down all public discourse. The right for Christians to speak publicly about Jesus Christ necessarily means that those of other belief systems will be equally free to present their truth claims in an equally public manner.

This is simply the cost of religious freedom. As the apostle Paul made clear in writing to the Corinthians, the preaching of the gospel has always been considered *offensive* by those who reject it. When Paul spoke of the Cross as *"foolishness"* and a *"stumbling block"* (SEE 1 Corinthians 1:23), he was pointing to this very reality – a reality that would lead to his own stoning, imprisonment, and his eventual execution.

Paul did not want to offend people on the basis of anything other than the cross of Christ and the essentials of the Christian faith. For this reason, he would write to the Corinthians about becoming *"all things to all people, that by all means I might save some" (1 Corinthians 9:22).*

It is a sad commentary that, many Christians manage to be offensive for reasons other than the offense of the gospel. This is to our shame and certainly to the injury of our testimony and gospel witness. Nevertheless, there is no way for a faithful Christian to avoid offending those who are offended by Jesus Christ and His Cross.

The truth claims of Christianity, by their peculiarity, and exclusivity, are inherently offensive to those who would demand some other gospel (SEE Galatians 3:1).

CHAPTER 12
"FROM TOLERANCE TO TOLERANCE"

The subject that I have selected for this chapter captures the essence of the word, "tolerance." The teachings of the term, tolerance as many other words of the English language, goes far beyond the traditional definition of the word.

Webster's dictionary defines *tolerate* as "to recognize and respect (others' beliefs, practices, etc.) without sharing them," and to bear or put up with (someone or something not especially liked).

"The apostle Paul expresses this attitude,

"....... bears all things .... endures all things" (1 Corinthians 13:7).

The Bible also tells us to, "Live in harmony with one another. If it is possible, as far as it depends on you, live in peace with everyone" (SEE Romans 12:16, 18). We are told to "accept one another, then, just as Christ accepted you, in order to bring praise to God" (SEE Romans 15:7). The Word of God distinctly tells us how Christians are to act toward each other and toward those outside the faith. (SEE Ephesians 4:2,32; Colossians 3:13; Galatians 6:10).

From Tolerance (Traditional)

The traditional tolerance defined above, as you can see is perfectly compatible with scriptural mandates. Respecting and protecting the legitimate rights of others, even those with whom you disagree and those who are different from you. In so many words, traditional tolerance means "everyone has a right to his own opinion." Traditional tolerance can be credited with having to do with the successful execution of many historical events, such as the abolition of slavery, the Civil-rights movement in the United States and in other parts of the World. As Christians, we are not required to compromise our godly principles to achieve peace, but it does mean,

"If it is possible, as much as depends on you, live peaceably with all men" (Romans 12:18).

Traditional tolerance values, respects, and accepts the individual without necessarily approving of or participating in his or her beliefs or behavior. Traditional tolerance differentiates between what a person thinks or does and the person himself.

But as I stated at the outset, today's definition and the concept our children are being taught in schools, our universities, and through the media is *vastly* different.

To Tolerance (Postmodern)

I would estimate that more than 90% of the time when you hear the word *tolerance* used outside of the church today, by college professors, schoolteachers, media, government officials, activists, celebrities, and probably, your own children – it almost never refers to traditional tolerance but to what I am calling *postmodern tolerance.*

The foundational tenet of postmodernism says, truth is relative; and therefore there can be no absolute or objective truth. This idea is a direct attack on traditional values. Therefore, all traditional tolerance is considered outdated. As stated earlier, postmodernism attacks the foundations of the modern era, as a failure.

This tolerance may sound like the traditional tolerance, but it is as different as day and night. Based on the *unbiblical* belief that "truth is relative to the community in which a person participates – while there are vast numbers of human communities -- there are many different so-called truths, and *all of them, subjective!* Now watch this, because understanding the outcome of this *unbiblical reasoning* is crucial. If all truth is up to humans – and all humans are "created equal" (as stated in the Declaration of Independence), then what logically follows? *This, all "truth" is equal.*

The Doctrine of Tolerance (Postmodern)

The doctrine of tolerance, believed and practiced by the majority is that all opinions are equal. Everyone's opinion has its point – therefore, all should be respected or praised. This means, there is no rational way to distinguish between them.

The definition of postmodern tolerance is that every individual's beliefs, values, lifestyle, and perception of *truth claims* are equal. Meaning, there is no hierarchy of *truth.* Your beliefs and my beliefs are equal – *and all truth is relative.*

Understand! This *unbiblical* tolerance is defined as the view that all beliefs, values, lifestyles, and perceptions of truth are equal. Now we can understand how the American courts operate the way they do – having embraced this definition by declaring that not only do "adherents of *all faiths* deserve equal rights as citizens," but "all faiths are equally valid as religions.

The Two tolerances in Contrast

In contrast traditional tolerance, which asserts that everyone has an equal right to believe or say what he or she think is right. Postmodern tolerance says that what every individual believes or say is equally right – equally valid. Hopefully, this understanding will help close the communication gap that we are experiencing because of the way our children are being taught to believe: All values are equal. All lifestyles are equal. All truth claims are equal. But they are not *equal!* (i.e. the ultra radical elements in this country).The Bible makes it clear that all values, beliefs, lifestyles, and truth claims are *not* equal. It teaches that the God of the Bible is:

The true God:

But the Lord is the true God; He is the living God and the everlasting King. At His wrath the earth will tremble, And the nations will not be able to endure His indignation (Jeremiah 10:10).

That all His words are true: *The entirety of Your word is truth, And every one of Your righteous judgments endure forever (Psalm 119:160).*

That if something is not right *in God's sight,* it is wrong:

And you shall do what is right and good in the sight of the Lord, that it may be well with you, and that you may go in and possess the good land of which the Lord swore to your fathers (Deuteronomy 6:18).

Notice, the Lord's view does not take sides – it is the truth according to God who rules over all cultures, as revealed in God's Word.

Wrong for One – Not Necessarily Wrong for Others

I was at a funeral recently, someone brought to my attention, girlfriends and boyfriends were listed on the obituary along with actual family members in the same manner as married couples. Some of them were members of local churches.

These are good, kind people, accomplished in life; who are living together and thinking nothing about it. They have absolutely no hang-ups about it. In a conversation with one couple, the woman responded, "it is our business and we aren't hurting anyone." This generation is different than yours. My generation is more tolerant. They said, 'Let people live the way they want to live.'

A 16 year old girl had a child out of wedlock. Some of the women of the church applauded her and gave her a baby shower in the dining hall. The circumstances surrounding the birth were never questioned nor investigated by the leadership.

If you observe, you'll notice that such views are *not* the exception today. Research indicates that, while less than half of the people of retirement age today believe that there is "no changing ethical standard of right and wrong," – about eighty five percent of children believe what postmodern tolerance is teaching: that what is wrong for one person is not necessarily wrong for someone else. And it is getting worse!

PART III

"HOW SHOULD WE THEN LIVE?"
CHAPTERS 13 – 15

CHAPTER 13
"FOR GOD SO LOVED"

For God so loved the world that He gave His only begotten Son, that whoever believes in Him should not perish but have everlasting life (John 3:16; also Genesis 3:15,21).

The Son's mission is bound up in the supreme *love* of God for the evil, sinful *world* of humanity that is in rebellion against Him. All of our love for Him should and does hinge on the word *"so."* It emphasizes the intensity of greatness of *His love* for us! The Father *gave* His unique and beloved Son to die on behalf of sinful men (think about that, you and me) – that we should receive *eternal life.*

For He made Him who knew no sin to be sin for us, that we might become the righteousness of God in Him (2 Corinthians 5:21). Eternal life refers not only to eternal quantity but divine quality of life. This life for believers in the Lord, Jesus, is experienced in our earthly life. In the verse above Paul summarized the heart of the gospel, resolving the mystery and explaining how sinners can be reconciled to God through Jesus Christ, *who knew no sin* (SEE 2 Corinthians 5:18-20).

How Shall We Live

What a tragedy it is that such an important ingredient as (*love*), is to our salvation, lifestyle and future destination – the world has distorted and downplayed its true meaning. Without loving God and our fellowman, our life is nothing. Jesus said,

"A new commandment I give to you, that you love one another; as I have loved you, that you love one another" (John 13:34).

Jesus speaks of it as the new commandment to love one another. It is new because it presents a new standard – the love of Jesus. Otherwise the commandment to love was not new, Deuteronomy 6:5 commanded love for God and Leviticus 19:18 commanded loving one's neighbor as oneself (SEE Matthew 22:34-40; Romans 13:8-10; Galatians 5:14; James 2:8).

However, Jesus' command in reference to love presented a distinctly new standard for two reasons:

(1) It was a sacrificial love *(agape)* modeled after His love "as I loved you" (SEE John 15:13).

(2) It is produced through the New Covenant by the transforming power of the Holy Spirit: (SEE Jeremiah 31:29-34; Ezekiel 36:24-26; Galatians 5:22).

"By this all will know that you are My disciples, if you have love for one another" (John 13:35).

That Christ would command us to love indicates that love is much more than a feeling or a preference; it is what we do and how we relate to others – *it is a decision, a commitment, and a lifestyle.* Jesus states that the world will know that we are His disciples if we love one another.

Schisms, disputes, unkind criticisms, and backbiting are contrary to the Spirit of Christ. His love was a sacrificial love. It was unconditional love. His love is constant and self-sustaining. His love provides for the best interests of the beloved, and He commands that we should love one another as He has loved us. Love is to serve as the distinguishing characteristic of discipleship (SEE 2 John 2:7-11; 3:10-12; 4:7-1-, 20,21).

Our Motivation

Some may tend to think, "I'll just love Jesus, and accept salvation by grace – then live however I wish and still reach heaven. However, God's word commands us to be fruitful. Jesus told His disciples,

"A good tree cannot bear bad fruit, nor can a bad tree bear good fruit. Every tree that does not bear good fruit is cut down and thrown into the fire. Therefore by their fruit you will know them" (Matthew 7:18-20).

In this Jesus said, that all who, receive the free gift of salvation ought to be overjoyed by sheer gratitude of what the Lord has done for them. Additionally, the apostle Paul tells us it's by God's mercies and our love for Him that we should be motivated, and dedicated to Christian service and living a fruitful life.

We do not serve Christ in order to receive His mercies, because we already have them (SEE Romans 3:21 – 8:39).

Even though you cannot earn your way to heaven, your wise choices, and service to others become the evidence of your commitment and transformation. Fear is a motivator due to the awesome power and unfathomable omniscience God possesses, but genuine zeal must be attributable to an intense desire to love, worship, thank and serve God for His goodness and greatness.

In the end, we surrender our lives to serve Him out of love and obedience. We further recognize that the kingdom of God is the major theme of what Jesus did and taught; therefore that should receive our highest commitment. (SEE Matthew 6:33).

I read a fiction story about a pig and a chicken walking down a sidewalk. Soon they passed a restaurant with a "ham and eggs" breakfast advertised in the window. The chicken began to speak proudly of their providing these entrees. The pig looked at the chicken and said, for your part it only takes a contribution; for mine it takes a commitment (my life)!

Understand that the kingdom is worth more than any other pursuit. Be ready to commit (your life) or forsake any personal goal that hinders entering into it. Recognize that kingdom people are childlike (not childish) in their faith, trust, and blameless, also pursue childlikeness in all interpersonal dealings. (SEE Matthew 13:44-52;18:1-5; Mark 9:33-27; Luke 9:46-48).

CHAPTER 14
THE GREATEST OF THESE IS LOVE

Considering prior chapters 1—13, the question asked of Jesus faces us today. How should we then live? What is most important? He responded by saying,

"Here is the entire Old Testament in a nutshell. I'm going to summarize it for you. All the Law and all the Prophets can be condensed into two tasks: Love God with all your heart, and love your neighbor as yourself." (Paraphrased) (SEE Matthew 22:37-40).

Every Christian is identified by what is important to them. What is most important? Considering what many televangelists are talking about today; and even many Christian books written – our conclusion would probably be "faith." However, the one great need in our Christian life is love, more love to God and more love to each other. Faith is activated by love.

In the Book of First Corinthians, chapters12 – 14, Paul, the apostle, gives us a word picture of love. In chapter 12, he lists our gifts; and in chapter 14, he explains how we are to operate these gifts of service in the kingdom of God. Reading those chapters readily brings into view the impossibility of effective service – unless we pass through chapter 13; where we are told, "the greatest of these is love." Since the basis of all gifts is love, that spirit of love is the qualifying factor for biblical exercise of the gifts of the Holy Spirit.

Of faith, Paul declares,

"If I have all faith, so that I can remove mountains, and have not love, I am nothing."

He concludes,

"And now abide faith, hope, and love, these three; but the greatest of these is love" (v.13).

Without a moment of hesitation, his decision is – love is #1.Other heavyweights agree with Paul: the apostle

Peter says,

"Above all things have fervent love among yourselves" (1 Peter 4:8).

The apostle John goes a step further and adds,

"God is love"(1 John 4:8).

The apostle Paul is also credited with the profound statement, *"Love is the fulfilling of the Law" (Romans 13:10).*

In those days, as well as today, we have those who declare they can get to heaven through keeping the Ten Commandments; however, the Scriptures claim about 304 more laws; which they fabricated from these ten. Jesus said breaking one of them made them guilty of all of them. Indicating the keeping of every law was impossible; however, "He said if you *love,* you will unconsciously fulfill all of them."

Notice what the Lord is saying. Take any of the commandments. If a man loves God, you don't have to tell him: ***"You shall have no other gods."*** Nor would he ever think of ***"Taking His name in vain."*** Love would fulfill all of these laws regarding God. By the same token, if he loved man as himself, he would not have to be told to honor his father and mother. His love for them would allow nothing less. Loving his neighbor would negate any thought of coveting what belongs to his neighbor.

You would only insult him by telling him he should not steal from or bear false witness against his neighbor. If he loved his neighbor – these things would not cross his mind.

Characteristics of Love

1. It **suffers long** – is patient (1 Thessalonians 5:14)

2. It is **kind** – gentle especially with those who hurt (Ephesians 4:32)

3. It **does not envy** – is not jealous of what others have (Proverbs 23:17)

4. It **does not parade itself** – put itself on display (John 3:30)

5. It is **not puffed up** – arrogance, or proud (Galatians 6:3)

6. It **does not act rudely** – mean-spiritedly, insulting others (Ecclesiastes 5:2)

7. It **does not seek its own** – way, or act pushy (1 Corinthians 10:24)

8. It is **not provoked** – or angered (Proverbs 19:11)

9. It **thinks no evil** – does not keep score on others (Hebrews 10:17)

10. It rejoices not **in iniquity** – takes no pleasure when others fall into sin (Mark 3:5)

11. It **rejoices in the truth** – is joyful when righteousness prevails (2 John 4)

12. It **bears all things** – handles the burdensome (Galatians 6:2)

13. It **believes all things** – trusts in God no matter what (Proverbs 3:5)

14. It **hopes all things** – keeps looking up, does not despair (Philippians 3:13)

15. It **endures all things** – puts up with everything; does not wear out (Galatians 6:9)

16. It **never fails** – the only thing it cannot do is fail (1 Corinthians 16:14)

The gifts of the Spirit, as wonderful as they are, are temporary and incomplete. They are for this age, while we are children (v.11). But **love** continues into the age to come: it is eternal, complete and fulfilling. The Scriptures differentiate between being dependent upon God, or childlike; and being childish or immature (SEE Matthew 16:3).

A more excellent way is not a negative comparison between gifts and love, since the temporal adverb **yet** indicates the continuation of the subject. All manifestations of the Spirit must at the same time manifest the ways of love, for love is the ultimate issue behind all things

CHAPTER 15
THE RIGHT HAND OF
GOD (BODY LIFE)

Like many pastors, I've invested many years of my adult life in ministry, with the hope and belief that if I preached well, prayed hard, and loved the flock deeply, the church that I pastor would reach its full potential.

But after more than 28 years as a pastor, nine church plants, founding a Bible College consisting of thirteen campuses located across a five-State area, and a training center in Accra, Ghana, West Africa. Add to that having served in both small and large venues, I've come to believe that the single biggest barrier to churches reaching their potential is this: the pastor-centered model of ministry.

The End of Pastor-Centered Churches

Let's face it ladies and gentlemen if churches are to realize their calling, we pastors must take a different approach to pastoral ministry. We must stop all this talking about equipping the saints, and start equipping the saints.

The typical church in America reflects the evolution of the pastoral model, whereby the pastor is the center of ministry – accompanied by a mind-set that says, lay involvement is a support role; which enables the trained professionals to be the "real" ministers.

What is so appalling about this model is the fact that most of what we see practiced today cannot be backed by the New Testament. In Exodus 18, we find Moses modeling the very ministry style that is such a hindrance to effective pastoral ministry today. It was not good then and it's not good now.

God sent Jethro to speak wisdom: "What you are doing is not good." In other words, Moses, no one's questioning your call, your motives, or your gifting, but you cannot do it all. Jethro coaches Moses to appoint leaders to oversee groups of 10, 50, 100, and 1000, and to only take the most difficult cases himself. In the very next chapter, God declares that all of Israel, not just the Levites, will become priests.

A Call to do what Jesus Did

Instead of playing the large numbers game, Jesus hand-picked twelve uneducated non-clerics to fire up God's revolution. Most of His ministry involved training the twelve. Why? Because Jesus knew His time was limited. He had this one chance to get it done, so, *He reproduced Himself in others.*

We put too much effort into studying *what* Jesus said at the risk of overlooking *how* He conducted His ministry. Notice Jesus' method of pastoring was pouring Himself into a few who'd pour themselves into the many.

His method is well demonstrated in Acts 6, when the people began complaining to the apostles for more attention. In response, the apostles raised other ministers who would use their own gifts, so the apostles could be about their own.

Paul continues the equipping method in how he raised up local leaders. He taught the gifting of the saints in 1 Corinthians 12 and the operation of gifts in chapter 14. The Holy Spirit makes a very important point in that, we are gifted in chapter 12, but we cannot get to the operation of the gifts in chapter 14 without going through chapter 13, the *love* chapter. In Ephesians 4:11, he provided the first real job description (rather than titles) for pastors and other church government leaders: apostles, prophets, evangelists, and teachers.

In the New Testament, the church in the Book of Acts had a pretty fluid structure of government. It closely resembled the synagogue's method. There were now disciples, elders, deacons, and even apostles, who walked with Christ.

In Acts 15, we are given insight into the early church's government. Notice, their decision-making process: There are the witnesses of the apostles Paul and Barnabas; there are leaders such as James; and then there is the *"unity"* of the entire believing community. Any Bible believing church or ministry can find biblical support for their form of government in this chapter.

The word *"unity"* means: the quality or state of being or made one; oneness; a definite quantity or combination of quantities taken as one or for which 1 is made to stand in calculation; harmony; accord; and concord. A church's structure can either serve the church or bring it to a standstill.

Unity

Unity can be directly linked to structure. Churches must provide support to a large number of people, activities and resources. Therefore, structures have relational dynamics that can either be positive or negative. Ephesians 4:13 informs us, the goal of ministry is coming into "unity of the faith" or "oneness." Jesus assures us that achieving and maintaining this "oneness" was never intended to be carried out by human intellect and strength alone (SEE John14).

He also promised His disciples that even though He was leaving; they would never be left alone; and the Father would send the Holy Spirit who would dwell in them forever. This promise is applicable to the individual Christian today: He promised,

"And I will pray the Father, and He will give you another Helper; that He might abide with you forever – the Spirit of truth, whom the world cannot receive, because it neither sees Him nor knows Him, but you know Him, for He dwells with you and will be in you. I will not leave you orphans, I will come to you" (John 14:16-18).

"These things I have spoken to you while being present with you. But the Helper, the Holy Spirit, whom the Father will send in My name, He will teach you all things, and bring to your remembrance all things that I said to you"(John 14:25-26).

Trust in the Lord with all your heart, and lean not to your own understanding; In all your ways acknowledge Him, and He shall direct your paths (Proverbs 3:5-6).

We can better perfect (mature) the saints through obedience to the Word of God. Notice Ephesians 4:12-13:

For the perfecting of the saints, for the work of ministry, for the edifying of the body of Christ: till we all come in the unity of the faith, and of the knowledge of the Son of God, unto a perfect man, unto the measure of the stature of the fullness of Christ (vv. 12-13).

The writer did not say we're to do the work of ministry *for* the saints, but rather prepare, equip the saints to use *their gifts* in serving others.

Structures in Today's Church

In most churches in America today, government structure consists of committees, or boards, policies, and majority rule.

These boards and committees are used to provide overall leadership and direction for the church. Such boards can be made up of elders, deacons, stewards, or other leaders, but the idea is that a small group of people provide oversight to the entire church. Another fallacy is the fact that those who do the ministry many times have no input to the "what and how to" of the mission.

Policies are written guidelines and rules that are intended to govern the decision making of the church. Many in the form of constitutions, and by-laws, designed to lay out a system of instructions and regulations that will ensure the proper operations. The danger with policies is there are never enough to cover everything that come up; and secondly, they can become an end unto themselves.

Finally, in the government structure of most churches is some form of majority rule. Whether it is the monthly business meeting or simply how a committee or board makes a final decision – the democracy of majority rule is often injected. The big problem with majority rule is that the majority does not always constitute the spiritually mature saints; therefore can be misleading.

Committees, policies, and majority rule are foundational within the life of the church. Yet, neither of the three is biblically based.

God's Multiplication Ministry

God's plan for adding to the church involves equipped saints. **(SEE Appendix II).**The apostle Paul demonstrates the methodology of the plan in his charge to Timothy:

"And the things that you have heard from me among many witnesses, commit these to faithful men who will be able to teach others" (2 Timothy 2:2).

The truth of God and salvation are established forever. Christ Jesus, the very Son of God Himself, came to earth to reveal God and the way of salvation. Witnesses down through the centuries confirm the truth. It is up to men to hear and receive it. A faithful Christian will hear, receive, and transmit the truth to others. He transmits the truth to others so that they in turn may teach others and pass the truth on down to future generations.

Note that the truth is to be committed to faithful believers. By faithful is meant a person who believes in Christ and in the Word of God – and who is loyal, reliable, dependable, and trustworthy. Therefore, a faithful Christian will not commit the truth to an unfaithful person.

Priesthood of Believers

But you are a chosen generation, a royal priesthood, a holy nation, His own special people; that you may proclaim the praises of Him who called you out of darkness into His marvelous light" (1 Peter 2:9).

Peter echoes Exodus 19:4-6, to remind us that we are to be a kingdom of priests. God gives Moses some specific directions concerning His *purpose* for Israel. Here God called Israel to be a "kingdom of priests and a holy nation," a people set apart exclusively for God. Now what does that mean to be a priest? What will be the function of a priest? Certainly the first function would be to minister to God, and secondly to minister to the people for God. In many ways, a priest is a mediator, a go-between for the people in their relationship with God. Every priest has a group or a specific area of responsibility.

The church today has the same priestly function with relation to the world. The priesthood of the believer is one of the major doctrines *restored* to the church. Notice again, we *are* to be a nation of priests, *not* a nation of lay persons who are *led* by priests. Every believer is equally a priest before God. This means that no mediator stands between us and God other than our High Priest, Christ Himself.

We have direct and ready access to the Father. Being a priest also means that we are responsible for *bearing witness* of Christ to others who need God's saving grace. Peter wrote that, as priests, our service to God is that of offering up spiritual sacrifices. These include the sacrifice of *praise* and *thanksgiving.* I believe these two are the natural outflow of the first and basic sacrifice – the surrender of our bodies to God as living sacrifices. Only when God has Lordship over our lives can He begin to place us into His *purpose*. The apostle Paul understood this priestly function of the believer. He told the Romans that because of God's grace toward him, he was a minister of Christ to the gentiles, ministering as a priest the gospel of Christ, that my offering of the gentiles might become acceptable, and sanctified by the Holy Spirit (SEE Romans 15:16).

The Protestant Reformation, which began in 1517, I believe was in reality a mighty move of God with the purpose of beginning a period of *restoration* of biblical truths lost during the so called "Dark Ages of the church." The Dark Ages spanned a period between the years 312 A.D. – 1517 A.D., when the Roman Catholic Church was the dominant depository of Christianity.

As with everything during these last days, God's mighty moves have accelerated the restoration process as the Lord builds His church, "without spot or wrinkle (SEE Ephesians 5:27). While there are no buildings in the New Testament named church; however, there are many images of the church in the New Testament; the most dominant are the body of Christ and the Spiritual house metaphors actually incorporating all the other is:

The Body of Christ

The image of the body promises the people of God as a physical body of people who truly are the continuation of all that Jesus began both to do and to teach (SEE Acts 1:1).

In Romans 5:12-21, the apostle Paul contrasts the "body of life, Christ" to the "body of death, Adam. Here we observe two humanities: (1). Those who stands with Adam and constitutes the body of death; will die twice (SEE Revelation 20:14). (2) Those who stand with Christ and constitute the body of life; will die once (SEE John 3:15).

This contrast presents a statement of truth, about the relationship that exists between Christ and His body. We come under the consequences of Adam's sin by our natural birth as his descendents. We come under Christ's obedience by faith and rebirth in Christ (SEE Romans 10:9-10; I Corinthians 15:22; 2 Corinthians 5:14).

The church is a new order, a new humanity, a new community which has the power to be an explosive force as the kingdom of God's presence in today's post-modern society. The church is called not to contain the message but to live its message – calling all people to repentance from the old body into the new body. I believe that the year 2000 marked the year of the restoration of the saints to their rightful place of kings and priests to the Most High God.

This radical shift pictures the church as the living organism; that it is. What do I mean by living organism? I mean that the church is the incarnation of Christ into the body of each born again believer (Romans 5:10). The apostle Paul selected the image of the human body to convey the organic manner in which the church is to function. The body is a functional whole made up of diverse parts all under the central coordination of the head. For example, the hands are for lifting; however, the left hand cannot command the right hand to help it lift a box. The signal to the right hand to help can only come from the head. There is no direct communications between the hands; or any other parts of the body except it be coordinated and signaled by the head. Notice Paul's conclusion:

"For as the body is one, and has many members, but all the members of that one body, being many, are one body so also is Christ" (1 Corinthians 12:12; also verses 13-27).

The church is a divine organism mystically fused to the living and reigning Christ, who continues to reveal Himself to the world and advance His kingdom in the people whom He has drawn to Himself. Paul is saying the church is a body under the control of its Head, Christ. What a tragedy it would be if the body refused to respond to the direction of its head. For example, a man bound to his hospital

74

bed, unable to control his body movements and functions due to nerve damage or disease damage to the brain. (SEE 1 Corinthians 12:27).

A church that is unresponsive to its Head is every bit as tragic and heartbreaking to watch (SEE Romans 12:5; Ephesians 5:30).

For the ministry of the whole body the Holy Spirit has bestowed various gifts. One term Paul uses to describe the gifts is *service*. Looked at from this perspective the gifts are a service for the church and the wider community. The gifts are not gifts to the individual Christian. They are gifts *through* the individual Christians. These spiritual gifts are resident in the Holy Spirit and when believers make themselves available, in word and deed, to be used of the Holy Spirit – it is for the glory of God. (SEE 1 Corinthians 12; Romans 12).

In the Book of Revelation, Jesus is presented in terms of His redeeming sacrifice, His resurrection, and His eternal reign: The apostle John wrote,

"And has made us kings and priests to His God and Father, to Him be glory and dominion forever and ever Amen" (Revelation 1:6).

The Chosen and His Chosen People

Like Paul, the apostle Peter also pictures Christ and the Christian assembled as one entity in the classic passage in 1 Peter 2:

Coming to Him as a living stone, rejected indeed by men, but chosen by God and precious, you also, as living stones, are being built up a spiritual house, a holy priesthood, to offer up spiritual sacrifices acceptable to God through Jesus Christ (vv. 4-5).

Though Israel nationally rejected Him, Jesus has become the Chief Cornerstone in God's new house. Accordingly, every Christian claimed by God, is a living stone and is **("Chosen"),** and belongs to a holy nation, set apart for a particular ministry. Each Christian has both a "kingship" and a "priesthood" of his or her own, to fulfill in their lives. Therefore each believer is raised to the status of "ministers." This puts all Christians in the role once performed by Old Testament priests.

Five-Fold Ministers

I believe these five gifts were given by Christ to the whole body of Christ as the official government leadership of the church. While Jesus was on the earth the five-fold ministry gifts were resident in Him and His ministry. However, when He ascended on high, He divided His mantle into five parts. These five gifts, apostle, prophet, evangelist, pastor, and teacher were restored to the body of Christ to complete all that Jesus began to do and to teach (SEE Acts 1:1).

A check of history reveals that the founders of this nation established the freedom of religion – free of Government intervention. However, at the time of the church's establishment in America; these truths established in Ephesians 4 were still concealed or distorted, as were many other biblical truths during the period 313 A.D. through 1517 A.D. During this period the church was Romanized by the Roman Emperor Constantine and his cronies. Most of the apostolic doctrine all but disappeared. In the absence of a proper model, many churches used secular models of leadership. As a result reliance upon the five senses, science and reason, "the Enlightenment," (power of the mind by which man attained truth and knowledge); which actually ran counter to the Restoration. One of the restored truths to the church during this same period was, *"The just shall live by faith" (Habakkuk 2:4).* In other words, the Christian is to live by a sixth sense (faith), of which the word of God is a component.

A New Order

The coming of Christ brought a whole *new order* to the church – an order that included both man and woman. Notice:

"There is neither Jew nor Greek, there is neither slave nor free, there is neither male nor female: for you are all one in Christ Jesus. And if you are Christ's, then you are Abraham's seed, and heirs according to the promise" (Galatians 3:28-29).

Rather than concerning our selves with gender; all Christians should concern themselves with the two philosophies of ministry encountered in the local church. First there are those who hold that truth is attained through science and reason, representative of Adam, who at best is incomplete.

Secondly, truth can only be attained through revelation knowledge. Therefore we engage our sixth sense (faith). Faith is needed as we humbly hear what the Spirit is saying to the churches. We better understand the mutual services God intends for the members of His body. **(SEE APPENDIX III)**

The Incarnation of the Christian (Christ in me) takes place in the salvation experience. In this way Paul summarizes the fact that the Christian in his or her totality, with Spiritual gifts and potentials, is to be employed in the service of the Lord. Because of God's mercies to us, Paul appeals to all Christians:

"I beseech you therefore, brethren, by the mercies of God, that you present your bodies a living sacrifice, holy, acceptable to God, which is your reasonable service. And do not be conformed to this world, but be transformed by the renewing of your mind. That you may prove what is that good and acceptable and perfect will of God" (Romans 12:1-2).

Since all things are for His glory, we must respond by offering ourselves for that purpose. Under the Old Covenant, God accepted the sacrifices of dead animals. But because of Christ's ultimate sacrifice, the Old Testament sacrifices are no longer of any effect (SEE Hebrews 9:11-12).

In light of all the spiritual riches believers enjoy solely as the fruit of God's mercies, it is logical that they owe God their highest form of service. Understood here is the idea of priestly service, which was such an integral part of Old Testament worship (SEE Romans 11:33, 36). We are not to be conformed, meaning, shaped in our thinking or accept any pattern of the godless system of this world whose god is the devil (SEE 2 Corinthians 4:4).

On the contrary, we are to be transformed, by a renewed mind committed to the ideals of the kingdom of God. Get rid of the "pig pen" thinking. Our minds will be transformed through the Word of God. If you get to know God's Word, and understand it clearly, you can know the will of God. The apostle Paul emphasizes putting off the old man and putting on the new man. Transformation is not only a work of discipline of the individual – but also from the work of the Holy Spirit. This requires us to move beyond the shallow living and venture out into the depths.

Paul speaks of the "God is at work in you concept" in Philippians 2:13; which focuses on divine influence. Then prior, there is the idea of "working out your own salvation," as mentioned in (v.12); which focuses on the ways, or disciplines, we use to work it out.

You don't need to run yourself through the many miseries and mine fields of life over and over again. We can learn through the experiences and earned wisdom of people who've already proven the answers to what you are struggling through with, now!

This is a necessary work of transformation/ discipleship. Hear, the psalmist,

Then I would not be ashamed, when I look into Your commandments. I will praise You with uprightness of heart (Psalm 119:6,7). How can a young man cleanse his way? By taking heed according to Your Word (Psalm 119:9).Your Word is a lamp to my feet and a light to my path (Psalm 119:105)

APPENDIX I
REGENERATION AND
SANCTIFICATION

"Now may the God of peace Himself sanctify you completely; and may your whole spirit, soul, and body be preserved blameless at the coming of our Lord Jesus Christ" (1 Thessalonians 5:2). A major problem the local church faces today is people continuing to live sinful lives; convinced that their life and service are pleasing to God. This is the result of a worldview that embraces relativism (a philosophy that claims there is no absolute truth). Therefore, they dismiss such Scriptures as Psalm 66:18; 1 John 3:9; etc as being outdated or just an opinion; while continuing to live in known sin as if God is winking, "a go ahead."

Paul admonishes us in the Scripture above that the goal of regeneration (new life in Christ) is to bring the whole person back into right relationship with God. The apostle Paul wrote,

"Not by works of righteousness which we have done, but according to His mercy He saved us, through the washing of regeneration and renewing of the Holy Spirit" (Titus 3:5).

Here we are taught that the Holy Spirit renews men, or makes men new, and through this renewing of the Holy Spirit, we are saved.

Jesus taught the same thing in John 3:3-5: Jesus answered and said unto him,

"Most assuredly, I say unto you, unless one is born again, he cannot see the kingdom of God. Nicodemus said to Him, "How can a man be born when he is old? Can he enter a second time into his mother's womb and be born again? Jesus answered, "most assuredly," I say to you, unless one is born of water and the Spirit, he cannot enter the kingdom of God."

What is regeneration? Regeneration is the impartation of life (spiritual life) to those who are dead (spiritually) through their trespasses and sin (SEE Ephesians 2:1). It is the Holy Spirit who imparts life. The apostle Peter explains how:

"Having been born again, not of corruptible seed but incorruptible, through the Word of God which lives and abides forever" (1 Peter 1:23).

In James we read,

"Of His own will He brought us forth by the word of truth, that we might be a kind of firstfruits of His creatures"(James 1:18).

These passages clearly point out that it is the Word of God that the Holy Spirit uses in regeneration, but it is only as the Holy Spirit uses the Word that the new birth results.

"It is the Spirit who gives life; the flesh profits nothing. The words that I speak to you are spirit, and they are life" (John 6:63).

Note the process of regeneration, **figures 1 – 4 below:**

Figure #1 shows that the whole person is spirit, soul, and body. Therefore in regeneration all three components, shattered and alienated from God by sin, must be reconciled with the Father, through the Son, by the Holy Spirit.

FIGURE #1

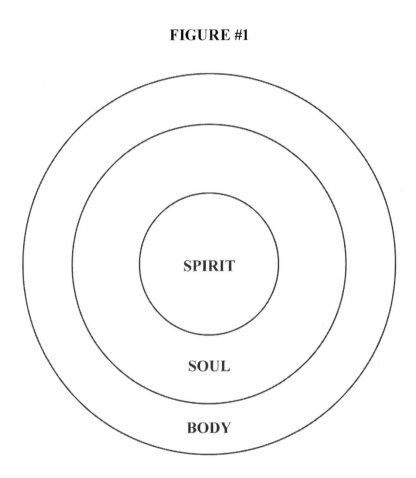

Figure #2: Regeneration begins as our spirit is quickened (made alive) by the Holy Spirit, through the Word of God. That, results from His drawing us, our repentance and acceptance of Jesus Christ as our personal Savior. At which time, we are reconciled to God by grace through faith in the finished work of our Lord and Savior, Jesus Christ alone (SEE Isaiah 53:11; Romans 10:9-10; 14:16-17, 26).

FIGURE #2

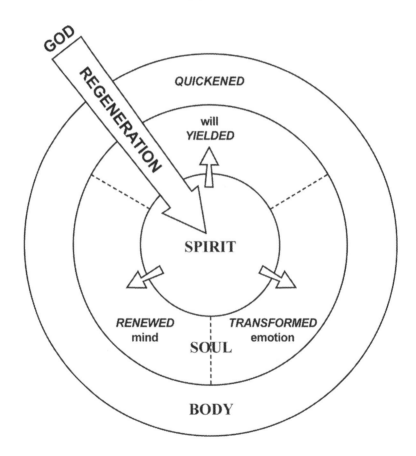

Figure #3: Notice, the size of the spirit in figure #3 is larger than that of figure #2. This is the results of the spirit (now indwelt by the Holy Spirit) taking back it rightful place; which was taken over by the soul as a result of the spirit being dead because of sin. (SEE Genesis 1:26-28; 3:1—Romans 5:6-21; 6:15-23). In the process of being reconciled to God, we undergo a transformation guided through spiritual progression wherein we are changed. Paul tells us,

"Now hope does not disappoint, because the love of God has been poured out in our hearts by the Holy Spirit who was given to us" (Romans 5:5).

Please notice, we now have the love of God and the Holy Spirit in our hearts. Regeneration then, is the impartation of a new nature, God's own nature, to the one who is born again (SEE 2 Peter 1:4). Our renewed soul reflects our new nature. Our minds, which were blind to the truth of God (SEE 1 Corinthians 2:14), are now renewed through the Word of God (SEE Romans 12:1-2; 1 Corinthians 13:1-8). Our will is in harmony with God's will (SEE John 4:34; 6:38; Galatians 1:10).

FIGURE #3

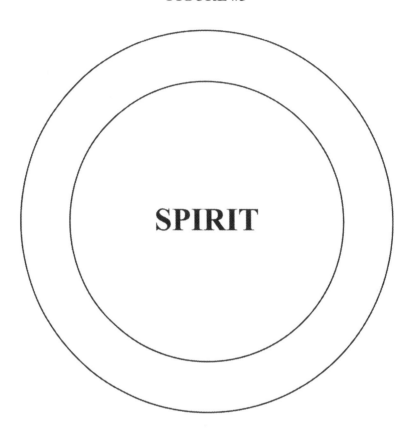

SPIRIT

As we begin a practice of our daily disciplines of studying God's Word, prayer, and meditation, our souls (mind, will, and affections) are renewed. The children of the church use to sing, *"Read your Bible and pray every day and you grow, grow, grow – don't read your Bible and pray everyday and you shrink, shrink, shrink"* – what truth! Our spiritual growth in Christ and commitment to Him in service is certainly impacted by our faithfulness to our daily disciplines. Some people become spiritual giants in a short period of time; while others remain spiritual dwarfs throughout their lives. While time is in the Lord's hands, we can certainly hinder our spiritual progression in the process of sanctification through our own interruptions of God's plan for our lives (SEE Romans 6:12-14; 1 Peter 2:24-25; 4:1-2).

The soul (flesh) comprises the mind, will, and emotions. Either one or all of these entities can become a great hindrance to wholeness, the goal of regeneration. Before Adam sinned, his spirit was in right relationship with God, Who is Spirit. Therefore, their communications were spiritual. The entrance of sin caused the death of Adam's spirit; which was his (spiritual) connection to God and the only way of communicating with God. At "new birth," it is the spirit of man that is "born again" and brought back into right relationship With God, through the saving work of Christ (SEE 2 Corinthians 5:21).. **Figure #4:** While the spirit has been born again, the soul and body must be renewed through the process of sanctification. In the process of sanctification both God and man has a part (SEE Romans 7:5-12; 12:1-3; Philippians 2:12-13; 3:7-11).

FIGURE #4

CLOSED   OPEN

The apostle Paul admonishes,

"I beseech you therefore, brethren, by the mercies of God that you present your bodies a living sacrifice, holy, acceptable to God, which is your reasonable service. And do not be conformed to this world, but be transformed by the renewing of your mind, that you may prove what is that good and acceptable and perfect will of God" (Romans 12:1-2)

.Transformation for kingdom living and service begins with a "renewed mind." The mind is the conduit through which God works transformation (sanctification) or renewal of the soul.

"As a man thinks in his heart, so is he" (Proverbs 23:7; also John 17:17).

We must begin to view reality from God's perspective. The Word of God is the key to the renewing of our minds. We hear the Word and receive it through our will. Remembering that the Word of God is the "Incorruptible Seed" (SEE 1 Peter 1:23), our willingness and receptiveness of that "Seed" indicates that we are "good ground." The seed grows in our spirit and cleanses (sanctifies our souls) us from the inside out (SEE John 17:17). The Bible says,

"For the word of God is living and powerful, and sharper than any two-edged sword, piercing even to the division of soul and spirit …" (Hebrews 4:12).

The word of God so to speak draws a piercing demarcation line between our spirit and soul. Our Holy Ghost filled spirit grows the seed of the Word which renews our souls and bodies. (What a harvest!) Transformed from the inside out, through the Truth of God's Word (SEE John 17:17; Ephesians 5:24; Romans 12:2).

FIGURE #5

HEART

Figure #5: The Word of God dwelling in us through the indwelling Spirit of God has transformed our total being. The story's told of an Eskimo, who owned two fighting dogs, one gray and one brown. Each Saturday afternoon, in the village center, he'd take bets on which dog would win in a race. The dog he chose won each time. Asked some time later, how this was possible, he replied, "the dog I feed always wins." Constantly, feeding the total person on study, meditation and application of God's word and His will, brings us into spiritual maturity (discipleship); which is the goal of regeneration. For we have the mind of Christ (SEE1Corinthians 2:16).

"There is therefore now no condemnation to those who are in Christ Jesus, who do not walk according to the flesh, but according to the Spirit" (Romans 8:1).

Normally the word "therefore" marks the conclusion of the verses immediately preceding it. But here it introduces the staggering results of the truth of Paul's teaching in the first seven chapters; that reconciliation is by faith alone on the basis of God's overwhelming grace.

"No condemnation" – "condemnation" is used exclusively in judicial settings as the opposite of acquittal. It refers to a verdict of guilty and the penalty that the verdict demands. Listen now! No sin a true believer can commit, past, present, or future can be held against him or her since the penalty was paid by Christ and righteousness was imputed to the Christian in Christ Jesus. This individual does not walk according to the flesh or the five senses; but walks according to the Spirit through our 6th sense, faith (SEE Romans 8:4, 9-14).

"Walk" refers to our lifestyles, our habits of living and thinking that characterize our lives (SEE Luke 1:6; Ephesians 4:17; 1 John 1:7). Our walk also expresses daily conduct, since every Christian is indwelt by the Holy Spirit, who has shed the love of God in our hearts, therefore, we will manifest the fruit they produce in our lives:

"But the fruit of the Spirit is love, joy, peace, longsuffering, kindness, goodness, faithfulness, gentleness, self-control. Against such there is no law. And those who are Christ's have crucified the flesh with its passions and desires. If we live in the Spirit, let us also walk in the Spirit" (Galatians 5:22-23).

"Fruit of the Spirit" – are Godly attitudes that characterize the lives of only those who belong to God by faith in Jesus Christ and are indwelt by the Spirit of God. The Spirit produces fruit which consists of nine characteristics that are without a doubt linked with each and are commanded of the true Christians throughout the New Testament:

1. **Love** – The Greek term is *"agape"* is the love of choice, referring not to emotional affection, physical attraction, or a familial bond, but to respect, devotion, and affection

that leads to willing, self-sacrificial service (SEE John 15:13; Romans 5:8; John 3:16-17).

2. **Joy** – is happiness based on unchanging divine promises and kingdom realities. It is the sense of well-being experienced by one who knows all is well in his or her relationship with God. That is, joy, in spite of favorable or non-favorable life circumstances (SEE John 16:20-22).

3. **Peace** – is the inner calm that results from confidence in one's saving relationship with Christ. Like joy, peace is not related to one's circumstances of life (SEE John 14:27; Romans 8:28; Philippians 4:6-7, 9).

4. **Longsuffering** – refers to the ability to endure injuries inflicted by others and the willingness to accept irritating or painful people and situations (SEE Ephesians 4:2; Colossians 3:12; 1 Timothy 1:15-16).

5. **Kindness** – is tender concern for others, reflected in a desire to treat others gently, just as the Lord treats all true Christians (SEE Matthew 11:28-29; 19:13-14; 2 Timothy 2:24).

6. **Goodness** – is moral and spiritual excellence manifested in active kindness (SEE Romans 5:7; 6:10; 2 Thessalonians 1:11).

7. **Faithfulness** – is loyalty and trustworthiness (SEE Lamentations 3:22; Philippians 2:7-9; 1 Thessalonians 5:24; Revelations 2:10).

8. **Gentleness** – also translated "meekness" is a humble and gentle attitude that is patiently submissive in every offense, while having no desire for revenge or retribution.

9. 9) **Self-control** – is the restraining of passions and appetites (SEE 1 Corinthians 9:25; 2 Peter 1:5-6).

APPENDIX II
THE MAKING OF A DISCIPLE

And Jesus came and spoke to them saying, "All authority has been given unto Me in heaven and on earth. Go therefore and make disciples of all nations, baptizing them in the name of the Father and of the Son and of the Holy Spirit, teaching them to observe all things that I have commanded you; and lo, I am with you always, even to the end of the age" (Matthew 28:18-20).

The four gospel writers viewed Christ from different aspects: Matthew's theme is Christ, the King; Mark's theme is Christ, the Servant; Luke's theme is Christ, the Son of man; and John's theme is Christ, the Son of God. It seems fitting then, that Matthew pen Jesus' final commission to His disciples. The humiliated Servant is now exalted Lord, King of kings having received the authority promised in (Daniel 7:14).

Make Disciples! Go, and as you are going, make disciples of all nations (people groups); seal their allegiance to Christ, and as witnesses to the world, by water baptism ministered under the authority of the Father, Son, and the Holy Spirit. Then teach them what Jesus has commanded you; and be assured of Christ's presence as you go divinely on your mission.

Because making disciples is a #1 priority for God, satanic interference is a high priority for the kingdom of darkness and certainly it is to be expected. Satan's diabolical schemes are found at every socio-economic level of our society. Watch out for him as his evil intensifies, for he realizes that he has but a short time left (SEE Revelation 12:12).

Before we go any further, perhaps we should get an understanding of just what a disciple is. As a spiritual parent and disciple-maker, I grieve when I observe the many claimants; who in reality left too soon for the mission (without proper training and spiritual growth). As a result, much of the foundational dogma and biblical doctrines are omitted when stating or practicing their philosophy of ministry (SEE Hebrews 5:12-13).

The Greek term for disciple in the New Testament is *mathetes* which means "learner." Once a person accepts Christ as their personal Savior, the goal is for them to grow to spiritual maturity, through learning to become Christlike. This requires a radical change in all aspects of his or her life. Disciple-making is a timely process; which requires the utmost dedication to duty on the part of the disciple-makers. Sadly, this is not a priority with many of our churches today.

There are several possible reasons for this short-fall, perhaps the church leaders lack the knowledge, skills, and resources to develop healthy, maturing disciples of Christ. That can and should be changed. If leaders prayerfully seek to become more mandate – conscience about making disciples, (mature Christians who *practice "the truth," share that faith, and reproduce their faith in others)* --- (SEE 2 Timothy 2:2; Jude 3).

The Mustness of Discipleship

Jesus said, *"If you abide in Me and My Words abide in you, you will ask what you desire, and it shall be done for you" (John 15:7).*

Certainly this verse indicates a timely process. According to the Webster Dictionary, the word "abide" means to live in; to dwell, signifying a relationship that moves from childhood through adulthood or maturity in this particular case. So to receive what you ask for, your personal relationship with Christ must be solidly established.

A Disciple (Mature Christian)

He or she must be born again and developing a healthy relationship with Christ.

He or she must be sanctified (set apart from the world and set apart unto God), and be full of the Holy Spirit (Word cleansed and Spirit – led) (SEE John 17:17; 14:13-15; Ephesians 5:18).

He or she must be teachable (SEE 2 Peter 1:2-4; Matthew 6:33).

He or she must realize that discipleship has a growth process; which involves a mix of human discipline with God's grace (SEE Philippians 2:12-13).

He or she must be developing spiritual disciplines (2 Timothy 2:15).

He or she must have a deep love for God and fellowman (SEE Matthew 22:37).

He or she must have a daily diet of Bible study, prayer, submission and realize the kingdom of God to develop the inner man (SEE Psalm 119:173-175; Matthew 6: 9-13, 33).

He or she must have a daily submission to God's will in service to develop the outer man (SEE Romans 12:1-2).

He or she must have a commitment to corporate worship, confession, and counsel (SEE Hebrews 10:25).

He or she must have a heart knowledge of right doctrine with conviction (SEE John 8:32).

He or she must have a rich knowledge of the Word of God with a great personal application of it (SEE Psalm 119:10-11; Proverbs 3:5-6; 2 Timothy 2:14-17).

What a Disciple "Looks Like"

Jesus specifically gave points of reference as to what makes someone His disciple. To Jesus, discipleship was following Him, not just His principles, ideas, or philosophy. He framed up His comments by saying, "Without this, you cannot be My disciple.

Discipleship to Jesus was a concrete relationship with Him; which would result in "knowing Him" – do you get the picture? In the Old Testament, we read, Adam "knew" his wife and she bore a son. Cain "knew" his wife, and she conceived (SEE Genesis 4:17, 25). So "knowing" Christ requires *intimacy,* in that, in this *relationship* there will be a *conception,* and later a *birthing* of (your maturity and your ministry of making disciples – through reproducing yourself in others (discipleship). (SEE 2 Timothy 2:2). Making disciples is so important to Christ that a crown of rejoicing has been set aside for those who excel in this task. Commitment and conviction are characteristic of Jesus' expectation of a disciple.

Commitment (Justification)

Most assuredly, I say unto you, unless one is born again, he cannot see the kingdom of God (John 3:3; also vv. 5-7).

If anyone comes to Me and does not hate his father and mother, wife, and children, brothers and sisters, yes, and his own life also, he cannot be My disciple. And whoever does not bear his cross and come after Me cannot be My disciple (Luke 14:26-27; 9:23-24).

Jesus gave Himself wholly to His cause and to His men. Therefore, He could ask the same of them. His call for commitment manifested in two aspects, it exposed the uncommitted and the committed. Disciples of Christ must be committed to the person of Christ, only. With Christ, everything hung on who He was and today who He is. You can follow His teachings without "knowing" Him; and therefore never be able to imitate Him.

For the most part, being a true Christian requires being interdependent. However, discipleship is the exception. We can only be disciples, individually. We must realize that personal responsibility and accountability are required in developing individual discipleship. No matter the methodology. It has to bring discipleship down to the personal level of each person. God made each of us to be unique. When I entered the Army I was issued a serial number by which I was identified. All of us became a number. With Christ, I am unique individual. Praise God! God *still seeks* for an individual man or woman to make up the wall and stand before Him on behalf of the land (SEE Ezekiel 22: 30).

The Cost of Commitment

Jesus said, *"Come unto Me, all you who labor and are heavy laden, and I will give you rest. Take My yoke upon you and learn from Me, for I am gentle and lowly in heart, and you will find rest for your souls. For My yoke is easy and My burden is light" (Matthew 11:28-30).*

In this passage, Jesus has given us two symbols of commitment. The first symbol, the cross is very familiar to us. Some people wear it as jewelry; however, I've never seen a yoke worn as jewelry. Yet the yoke is just as much a symbol of commitment as the cross. He said,

"......Whosoever will come after Me, let him deny himself, and take up his cross and follow Me" (Mark 8:34).

"Take My yoke upon you, and learn of Me ...." (Matthew 11:29)

Put together, we have a picture of what Christian commitment is all about. We are ready to die on the cross or pull the yoke. We are ready to bleed or sweat; depending on whichever our Lord requires of us – so that His will be done on earth as it is in heaven.

Learn of Me

On the news the other day, I watched women in Haiti carrying sacks of food and other supplies on their heads. In many cases the load on their head was equal to almost one half of their body weight. My mind went back to my basic and advanced training in the Army. Part of that training included what was known as a "forced road march." In this case we had to carry a forty pound backpack on our backs. I entered training weighing 115 pounds, and this was on a very hot August day on "Tank Hill," at Fort Jackson, South Carolina. The march was about ten miles; however, I was in trouble after about three miles – as that forty pounds began to take its toll, I began to think about falling out of the road march. I struggled on thinking of how important it was to complete this phase of training. Soon it occurred to me; that I was not going to make it! At that very point I felt the pressure on my back ease up. My squad leader, who had been watching me all along, came a long side and lifted my pack up to a higher position where the weight was carried by my shoulders. Oh! What a relief! Please notice he did not physically take my back pack off of me, but he made carrying it easy. How? He *showed* me the proper way to carry it.

Undoubtedly, when the squad leader instructed us on how to carry a forty pound back pack, I wasn't paying attention nor did I read the book prior to taking off. By the time we reached the break area, I truly knew how to carry those forty pounds. I have carried that incident with me throughout life. I will never forget my squad leader's hand or his words.

Part of Jesus' invitation in this Scripture, bids us to: *"Learn of Me."* Commitment includes a "walking relationship." Everything hangs on the person of Jesus (Who He is) to us. His Word flows out of His person. We hear His instructions as the Holy Spirit speaks to our hearts and from His Word, the Bible. The Bible is our "How to" instructions that He left us. Many of us are falling out of the march, because we are not listening or reading the instructions without which we cannot know the person of Jesus Christ. That leaves us "with our own understanding only." What a disaster! Jesus left us many, many precious promises in the Bible. All of His promises were atoned on Calvary. In other words, they are already done. He has extended them to His followers through grace and we can access them through faith. For example:

"If you abide in Me, and My words abide in you, you will ask what you desire, and it shall be done for you. By this My Father is glorified, that you bear much fruit; so you will be My disciples" *(John 15:7-8).*

Abide means to "dwell or live in." This means a birth through adulthood (life) relationship. In this instance, from "re-birth" we grow to spiritual maturity (through living in Christ and His words living in us). The "much fruit" that our Father is looking for in His people is Christlikeness (SEE Galatians 5:22-23). Very often spiritual competence never develops because we don't heed the Apostle Paul's advice to Timothy,

"Be diligent to present yourself approved to God, a worker who doe not need to be ashamed, rightly dividing the word of truth" *(2 Timothy 2:15).*

This passage invites to apply the Scriptures by maintaining a clear conscience before God and man – by devoting yourself to responsible study of the Bible and meditation – become competent in interpretation of Scripture. Self-feeding skills are imperative for spiritual maturity. Any ministry that is concerned about making disciples will definitely encourage this type of Commitment – to grow as a *learner* of Jesus;

for without it, discipleship (spiritual maturity) cannot happen (SEE Matthew 6:33).

Conviction (Sanctification)

"You shall know the truth and the truth shall set you free" (John 8:32).

This knowing carries with it more than the cognitive; but also the keeping or applying of truth that marks a person as a disciple of Christ. Often we find that many Christians are very rich in knowledge – but very poor in application. Therefore, they pride themselves in having the "right" doctrine, even to having the ability to argue the truth of it – but without *conviction* – the kind that leads to spiritual maturity and discipleship. Our lifestyles differ very little from the cultural norm. True conviction leads to commitment.

Both Apostles Paul and Peter expounded on how this could best develop in the Christian, leading to discipleship. Each practiced a plan that proved effective in their ministries. Paul maintained the same plan throughout despite differing circumstance. His plan placed Christ as the foundation of the community; then he added three levels consisting of faith, hope and love. These four themes are interrelated and essential to spiritual maturity (SEE 1 Corinthians 3:10). Peter's plan reminds that spiritual maturity involves acquiring a divine nature (qualities that stem from Christ's character). He encouraged Christians to (build one virtue on top of another). "Make every effort to grow this way" (SEE 2 Pete1:5-8). It begins with personal conviction and it ends in sanctification – a disciple.

APPENDIX III
EVANGELISTIC RELATIONSHIPS

There are more churches today than ever before. Parachurch ministries are flourishing. More Christian resources are available to the churches than could ever be read or applied. Pastors' libraries are loaded with "how to" books on the unchurched and how to win them to faith in Jesus Christ.

Yet, many churches struggle to be change agents for their local communities. Each year statistics show that thousands of churches fail to baptize even one convert to Christ. It is reported that over 2.5 million people die each year in this country. Only God knows how many of those people will spend eternity separated from God. Researchers estimate that over 65% of these people will go into eternity without Christ.

Many of these people were denied the opportunity to learn about the saving grace and knowledge of our Lord and Savior, Jesus Christ – because nobody took the time to introduce them to a living and eternal God. This is a sad commentary and it undermines the Scriptural mandates of the gospel that says,

"Go and make disciples of all nations, baptizing them in the name of the Father and the Son and of the Holy spirit, and teaching

them to obey everything I have commanded you ...." Matthew 28:19-20).

Having served as pastor of churches in small and large venues during the past 28 years, I know the solutions are not easy. Jesus didn't promise His disciples that evangelizing the world would be easy. Notice, He instructed believers,

"The harvest is plentiful but the workers are few. Ask the Lord of the harvest, therefore, to send out workers into his harvest field" (Matthew 9:37-38).

Leaders are praying daily for the Lord to send out workers from their churches and paraministries into the harvest fields. The sad reality is, *"the workers are few."* I believe it is the goal of every true leader to be a part of a committed and evangelistically highly active community where *every* member is faithfully participating in reaching out to the unchurched people. Perhaps, as pastors and teachers, we have neglected to teach with passion; that every Christian's first duty is their ministry of reconciliation. The Scriptures say to us,

"Now all things are of God, who has reconciled us to Himself through, Jesus Christ and has given us the ministry of reconciliation, that is, that God was in Christ reconciling the world to Himself, not imputing their trespasses to them and has committed to us the word of reconciliation" (2 Corinthians 5:18-19).

Those of us already reconciled, (v.17), have the mandate to carry the message to others. If we view this task from an earthy perspective – truly it is an impossible undertaking. I think too many of us preach *"all things are possible with God"*; but have a problem with application. First of all, Paul is talking to those "in Christ," a new creation; old things, (old attitudes, strongholds, worldviews, and other earthly perspectives) have passed away. Christ's death and resurrection for us, and our identification with Him by faith, make existence as a new creation possible. We can identify with him,

"I can do all things through Christ who strengthens me" (Philippians 4:13).

He bore our sins on the Cross and endured the penalty that we truly deserved,

"That we might become the righteousness of God in Him" (2 Corinthians 5:21).

Another vital part of the Great Commission is the personal promise of Jesus Himself, when He said,

"And surely I am with you always, to the end of the edge" (Matthew 28-20).

Also, just prior to His ascension into heaven, Jesus told Hid disciples,

"But you will receive power when the Holy Spirit comes upon you; and you will be my witnesses in Jerusalem, and all Judea and Samaria, and to the ends of the earth" (Acts 1:8).

Jesus promised to empower us and be with us every step of the way in our witnessing worldwide. That being true, why are we failing? Why are there so few laborers? As I stated in an earlier chapter, we can worship together, function as part of a team, but we can only be a disciple individually. In one of His ministry models, Jesus communicated to us:

"As He spoke these words, many believed in Him. If you abide in My word, you are My disciples indeed. And you shall know the truth, and the truth shall make you free" (John 8:30-32).

In v.29, for Jesus, doing the will of the Father was not an occasional choice in times of crisis. Rather, the Father's constant presence in His life magnified the fact that there never was a moment when He did not do the Father's will. Certainly, it would follow that we concern ourselves with His will as He did the Father's. Like the claim of many people to be descendents of Abraham was futile, because their lifestyle showed a lack of a personal relationship to Him (vv. 31-59). So, many in our churches claim to know Christ; however, there is little or no evidence of a personal relationship with Him to back their claim. If they were children of God, they would reverence and obey the Son of God.

Jesus said,

"If you love Me, keep My commandments" (John 14:15).

Those who love Christ will prove their devotion by their obedience. Jesus went on to say,

"If you keep My commandments, you will abide in My love, just as I have kept My Father's commandments and abide in His love" (John 15:10).

When we abide in Christ, our prayers are effective, we glorify God in our fruit-bearing, we demonstrate our discipleship, and we experience Christ's joy within us (vv. 7-11).

Jesus said,

"You shall love the Lord your God with all your heart, with all your soul, and with all your mind. This is the first and great commandment. And the second is like it: You shall love your neighbor as yourself these two commandments hang all the Law and the Prophets" (Matthew22:37-40).

Jesus summed up all moral responsibilities in the word *love,* expressed in the twofold direction of God and neighbor. One of the major hindrances to witnessing and making disciples in the local church is a lack of love for Christ and people. Added to these is a lack of teaching and application; which results in the biblical truths not being passed to the next generation (SEE Deuteronomy 6:4-5).

Paul admonished Timothy,

And the things that you have heard from me among many witnesses, commit these to faithful men who will be able to teach others also (2 Timothy 2:2).

Timothy was to take the divine revelation he had learned from Paul and teach it to other faithful men – men with proven spiritual character, fruitfulness, and giftedness; who would in turn pass on those truths to other faithful men. By faithful is meant a person who:

1. Believes in Christ and in the Word of God.

2. Is a servant of God's word; who boldly shares and demonstrates its message through fruitful living and the spoken word. He or she is careful and competent to communicate its truth with absolute accuracy.

3. Is loyal, reliable, dependable, and trustworthy.

4. Looks for faithful men people and commit the truth to them.

5. Realize that he or she must look at them self as a link between two generations.

To be an effective witness, we must have a ministry focus – and model Jesus' attitude as demonstrated in Luke 17:26-27:

"And as it was in the days of Noah, so it will be also in the days of the Son of man: They ate, they drank, they married wives, they were given in marriage, until the day Noah entered the ark, and the flood came and destroyed them all."

This situation is illustrated in below **FIGURE #6** the pie is cut into three segments; which I have numbered Groups #1, #2, and #3.

FIGURE #6

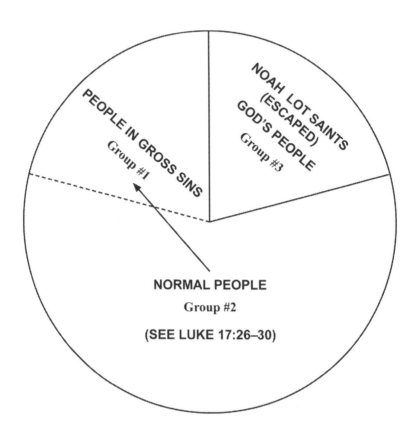

The people of **Group #1** are engaged in "gross sins" i.e. drugs, theft, pornography and other gross immorality. Much of our preaching, witnessing, and ministry today is aimed at this group and much of it takes the form of "thou shall not" or just plain legalism. A second and larger percentage of people **Group #2** are just normal people. as depicted in vv 26-27. They are drinking (perhaps tea or sodas), marrying, giving in marriage, building homes, and businesses, planting crops – all normal societal functions (not sins). So let's see how Jesus contrasts these two groups in Luke 17:26-30, we'll begin with **Group #2.** These were normal people; however – they placed these (normal) societal concerns above their relationship with Christ. So *"As in the days of Noah," –the flood came and destroyed them all* the situation is similar in America today. Group #2 people are considered normal, because they are good neighbors, moral in conduct, stable, employed, and in many instances pillars of the community and in some cases the church.

Yet, Christ and the things of Christ are not a concern to them. **Jesus Contrasts the two Groups** Notice, He did not address the "gross sins" (Group #1).The dotted line between Groups #1 and #2 indicate that they are really one and the same group. In verses 27 and 29, notice what is said of both groups, *"and destroyed them all"* They were destroyed due to a lack of righteousness. As I stated before many Group #2 people are in our churches; some leading ministries. God is no respecter of persons. Membership is not relationship and for many material things are the object of their worship and service instead of the living God. **Group #3,** people were delivered out before the destruction came. This is a wake-up call to the church. We work and live alongside these normal people everyday, some are our family members. In many cases, we already have an on-going relationship with them. This is a great opportunity for individual relational evangelism. Speak and live the truth before them in love – before its everlasting too late!

About the Author

Jay R. Leach is the president and co-founder of the Bread of Life Ministries International, with his wife of forty-seven years, Magdalene. The Leaches pastor the Bread of Life Christian Center and Church in Whiteville, North Carolina. They are the proud parents of five adult children, sixteen grandchildren, and six great-grandchildren.